Performing Arts Collections in the Nordic Countries

Denmark
The Faroe Islands
Finland
Greenland
Iceland
Norway
Sweden

Published by
NCTD – Nordisk Center for Teaterdokumentation
and The Royal Danish Library

Performing Arts Collections in the Nordic Countries

Denmark • The Faroe Islands • Finland • Greenland • Iceland • Norway • Sweden

Published by NCTD – Nordisk Center for Teaterdokumentation www.nctd.eu and The Royal Danish Library

Editor: Anna Lawaetz (alaw@kb.dk)

Editorial Team: Benedikte Berntzen, Magnus Blomkvist, Sigríður Jónsdóttir, Rikard Larsson, Marjaana Launonen, Birgit Kleist Pedersen

Translation: Steve Smith

Layout: Jakob K. Meile, The Royal Danish Library

Content

Introduction

This is the first overview of Performing Arts Collections in the Nordic Countries published in English from *Nordisk Center for Teaterdokumentation*. It is a register of archives, libraries, museums, theatres and institutions that hold performing arts records in their collections as well as a description of what the collections contain. Furthermore the main educational institutions are mentioned.

As a foreigner to Nordic languages, it can be difficult to access Nordic performing arts archives and get an overview over the field. The ambition with this publication is to make the archives accessible to a larger group of scholars all over the world.

For the first time in more than 40 years of publishing, we have included Greenland and The Faroe Islands in an overview over Performing Arts Collections in the Nordic countries. The performing arts tradition in these two countries still lack broader research. It is my hope, as editor in chief, that this inclusion will strengthen scholarly awareness of the performing arts history of both Greenland and The Faroe Islands in a broader context.

We live in a digital era, with access to a great deal of digital or digitized records. Unfortunately, web links die out quickly. Thus, the editorial choice has been to link to the main web page of each institution. Not all institutions have an English web site, but with the descriptions in this publication, it is our hope that it will be easier to access the collections listed in it.

The editorial team from Nordisk Center for Teaterdokumentation consists of Marjaana Launonen (Finland) Sigríður Jónsdóttir (Iceland), Benedikte Berntzen (Norway), Magnus Blomkvist and Rikard Larsson (Sweden), Birgit Kleist Pedersen (Greenland), and Anna Lawaetz (Denmark and The Faroe Islands).

Copenhagen, December 2023

Anna Lawaetz
Editor in chief
Research Librarian, PhD, The Royal Danish Library

Denmark

Illustration: De syv dødssynder (Die sieben Todsünden der Kleinbürger) by Bertolt Brecht. Choreography and director: Harald Lander. Set Designer: Svend Johansen. The Royal Danish Theatre, Copenhagen, 1936. Photographer: Holger Damgaard. The Royal Danish Library.

Billund Kommunes Museer

Billund Municipality Museums

ADMINISTRATION
Tinghusgade 15
DK–7200 Grindsted

EXHIBITION
Morsbølvej 102
DK–7200 Grindsted

CONTACT
+45 79 72 74 90
museet@billund.dk
www.billundmuseum.dk

Contains a special collection about fun fair and street entertainment around the town of Vorbasse, including the Mr Swing King carrousel, a circus wagon, the so-called Black Diamond (a travelling miniature of a German coalmine), and many artefacts concerning circus, street entertainment, and fun fairs.

Cirkusmuseet

The Circus Museum

ADMINISTRATION AND ARCHIVE
Alarmpladsen 3
DK–2650 Hvidovre

EXHIBITION
Hovedporten 6
DK–2650 Hvidovre

CONTACT
+45 36 49 00 30
info@cirkusmuseet.dk
www.cirkusmuseet.dk

The museums main collection stems from the juggler and collector, Ølund "Barly" Jacobsen. Among other things, it comprises thousands of various photographs, travel books, programmes, posters, materials connected to DAF (the Danish Artists Union), contracts, scrapbooks, correspondence, costumes, films, radio recordings and props. The collection contains items from the middle of the 1800s to today. The Museum continuously receives material connected to the circus, artists, and fun fairs. Thus, the museum also has the collection of the magician Truxa. Furthermore, the Museum also has a library with the most important publications regarding the circus, artists, and fun fairs.

Cirkusmuseet i Rold

The Circus Museum in the Village of Rold

POSTAL ADDRESS
Hobro Museum
Vestergade 23
DK–9500 Hobro

CONTACT
+45 99 82 41 70
historiskmuseum@aalborg.dk
www.nordmus.dk/u/cirkusmuseet

EXHIBITION
Østerled 1
Rold
DK–9510 Arden

The Circus Museum in Rold is housed in Circus Miehe's old winter quarters, which is Denmark's only preserved wooden circus building. The Museum provides an insight into the circus as a workplace during the past 200 years.

Designmuseum Danmarks Bibliotek

The Design Museum's Library

POSTAL ADDRESS
Bredgade 68
DK–1260 København K

CONTACT
+45 33 18 56 50
bib@designmuseum.dk
www.designmuseum.dk

Founded in 1890 by the Industrial Association with the purpose of spreading knowledge about Danish and foreign handicrafts, the industrial arts and design. The library contains literature on theatre history, scenography, masks, dance/ballet, shadow puppets, circus, marionette and puppet theatre. The picture collection contains theatre engravings (16th – 18th century), Danish decoration and costume drawings, Danish and foreign theatre and circus posters.

Det Danske Filminstitut

The Danish Film Institute

MUSEUM & CINEMA
Vognmagergade 10
DK–1120 København K

CONTACT
+45 33 74 34 12
bibliotek@dfi.dk
cinematek@dfi.dk
www.dfi.dk

The Museum is the home of the National Film Archive which contains a large collection of Danish and foreign films: approximately 26,000 films in all formats, both in negatives and positives. Since January 1998, the Museum has stored a copy of all films released on video in Denmark: about 1000 videos, primarily Danish and foreign feature films, Danish documentary material, TV dramas and series. The Museums documents department consists of a library for film and tv as well as a photo and poster archive. The library is the main library in this field with plays, periodicals, and press cuttings about tv and film.

Det Kgl. Bibliotek

The Royal Danish Library

The Royal Danish Library consists of several amalgamated libraries and collections which can be dated back to 1482. Since the year 2000, several public institutional merges have occurred which has affected both university libraries and national ones. The various merges mean that these libraries are all now a part of the Royal Danish Library.

In 1697, it became obligatory in Denmark to submit a copy of all books, newspapers, and other forms of printed materials to the Royal Danish Library. During the first 100 years the law was not particularly adhered to. The collection of published Danish materials thus lacks a number of publications. In 2005, a new law came into force which obligated the Royal Danish Library to collect material from the internet in its Net Archive.

LIBRARY CATALOGUE
www.soeg.kb.dk

CONTACT
+45 33 47 47 47
kontaktbibliotek@kb.dk
www.kb.dk

Det Kgl. Bibliotek – København

The Black Diamond

POSTAL ADDRESS
Søren Kierkegaards Plads 1
DK–1221 København K

Below is a list of the collections that have special relevance to the performing arts. Unless otherwise stated, they are all housed in The Black Diamond.

Det Kgl. Bibliotek, Teatersamlingen

The Royal Danish Library, The Theatre Collection

The Theatre Collection systematically collects plays from all Danish theatres as well as radio and tv plays. Since the majority of the material is unpublished, a large part of the collection has the status of an archive. The collection includes 14,000 printed texts and books, and approximately 22,000 performed unpublished plays. Among them are an entire collection of plays from, among others, Casino Teatret, Dagmarteatret, Nørrebros Teater, Folketeatret, Det Ny Teater, Betty Nansen Teatret etc., as well as collections from theatrical publishers and actors. Furthermore, there is a large collection from the Danish Playwrights Union. Dansearkiv.dk's collection of dance recordings and Odin Theatre's extensive archive are now part of the Theatre Collection. Hegermann-Lindencrone's tape archive with 2,700 hours of recordings of performances at Danish theatres from 1948–1988 is also a part of the collection. A more specific register of the collection – registered as unregistered – can be found on the website.

Det Kgl. Bibliotek, Musiksamlingen

The Royal Danish Library, The Music Collection

The collection consists of a main collection with both printed material and manuscripts along with a special collection consisting of, among others, the Royal Theatre's older collection of theatre music (opera, ballets, musical comedies, between scene music etc.). The collection also houses a large number of music archives from privately owned theatres. Furthermore, there is an orchestra library with material from performances.

Det Kgl. Bibliotek, Dansk Folkemindesamling

The Royal Danish Library, The Danish Folklore Collection

Through audio and video recordings, written material, and photos, the collection highlights ordinary people's stories, shows, music, dance, song and clapping games, myths, local history and reminiscences as well as the meaning and use of these from 1843 to the present day. The collection contains, among others, Anders Enevig's study collection of the history of the circus (including fun fairs in the Nordic countries), and recordings of traditional oral story telling.

Det Kgl. Bibliotek, Håndskriftsamlingen

The Royal Danish Library, The Handwritten Manuscript Collection

The collection includes more than four and a half kilometres of shelves of handwritten items (letters, plays, personalia, etc.) from the early Middle Ages to more recent times including a good deal of theatre related material.

Among this material can be mentioned, the Royal Danish Theatre's prompter archive (a contents list of this archive can be found under the signature Ms.phot. 247 kvart), letters, contracts, and proceedings from the Danish Dramatists Union, as well as documents concerning the Royal Danish Theatre as well as the history and repertoire of other Danish theatres. The collection also contains an extensive collection of letters, personalia, plays etc. from a wide range of actors, dancers, directors, and playwrights such as Johanne Luise Heiberg, Poul Reumert, Bodil Ipsen, August Bournonville, Harald Lander, and Flemming Flindt.

Det Kgl. Bibliotek, Kort- og billedsamlingen

The Royal Danish Library, The Collection of Maps and Images

Throughout the centuries, The Royal Library has collected images. Firstly, engravings, thereafter, photographs. Today, images are collected digitally. A large range of theatre related material is to be found in the collection. Recently Holger Damgaard's (1870–1945) 10.000 theatre photos from various theatres in Copenhagen taken by Holger Damgaard from 1909 to 1940 has been digitised. Not all of the items have been registered in the catalogue, but they can still be booked through kb@kb.dk.

- Klaus Lindewald (1935–1986). Extensive collection of positives and negatives from Lindewald's job as photography for a number of theatres in Copenhagen. The photos depict both the work up to a performance as well as the final result on stage. The positives and contact sheets are archived under the respective theatres and alphabetically after the name of the performance (among others, Det Ny Teater, Gladsaxe Teater, Folketeatret, Det Danske Teater).
- H. J. Mydtskov (1887–1973), Jørgen Mydtskov (1931–2011), and Rigmor Mydtskov (1925–2010). Theatre photographs during the period 1931–1964 taken by H. J. Mydtskov and his son Jørgen Mydtskov registered alphabetically.
- The Royal Danish Theatre. Various stage images from the Royal Theatre's archive. Arranged alphabetically.
- The Theatre Museum's Collection. Photographs from a number of performances at Danish theatres: Caféteatret (1969–1978, among others, from the French Studio and Theatre School), Casino (1916–1919), Dansk Skolescene (slides from Thomas P. Hjejle 1924–1938),

Helsingør Sommerteater (1914–1949), Det Kongelige Teater (1904–1960, including photographs of scenography and decoration as well as a large number of ballet photos), Det Ny Scala (1966–1972), Det Ny Teater (1908–1927), Folketeatret (ca. 1912–1930), Jørgen Blaksted Tour (1970–1998), Nørrebro (1980erne), Odense Teater (1896–1935), Rialto (1980–2005), Scala (1970–1983), Aarhus (1952–1963) plus individual performances from various theatres. Search the collection in: REX. Proveniens: Teatermuseet

- Danish photos and theatrical decorations. Views, scrapbooks, puppet theatre. A register of Alfred Jacobsen's publications exists.

In addition, the Museum for Danish Newspaper Cartoons has a large number of theatre drawings. The Royal Danish Library holds the digital part of the collection whereas the physical part has been moved to the museum Den Gamle By.

The National Collection of Photograpy has a number of theatre photos. They can be found here: www.kulturarv.dk/kid/VisMuseum.do?museumId=358.

In 'Diverse samlingen' can be found stage and stage setting photographs (see also for example: "Danske billeder", "dukketeaterdekorationer"), photographs of non-identifiable stage artists as well as theatre posters (these can also be found under Danske afdeling /Småtryk)

A number of theatre photos can also be found in some of the other of the Royal Library's collections (the newspaper archive among others). Some have been digitised and can be sought in the digital collection.

Det Kgl. Bibliotek, Småtrykssamlingen

The Royal Danish Library, The Collection of Pamphlets and Corporate Publications

The pamphlet collection is divided into a number of groupings, among them, Theatre. This includes programmes, reports, accounts, journals, articles of association etc. from individual theatres, ensembles, and their various associates (children's theatres, local theatres, touring theatres, open-air theatres, amateur theatres, revues, puppet theatres, and school theatres). In addition, this part of the collection contains items from theatre associations, professional associations, the Danish Actors Union, festivals, guest performances, theatre calendars and more. Not everything is registered in the catalogue. If you cannot find what you are looking for, you can write directly to the Collection of Pamphlets and Corporate Publications via kontaktbiblioteket@kb.dk.

Det Kgl. Bibliotek, Danmarks Kunstbibliotek

Danish National Art Library – Royal Danish Library

POSTAL ADDRESS
Postboks 2149
DK–1016 København K

ADDRESS FOR VISITORS
Nyhavn 2
DK–1051 København K
(Lending department)

ADDRESS FOR VISITORS
Transformervej 21B
DK–2860 Søborg
(Reading room, by appointment only)

CONTACT
dkb@kb.dk
www.kunstbib.dk
www.kb.dk
+45 33 74 48 02

Established in 1758. The main library for architecture, sculpture, painting, photography, art history, and museology. Amalgamated with the Royal Danish Library 1st January 2017. The collection contains books, periodicals, photographs, slides and architectural drawings, architectural models, and an archive collection of painters and architects including models and drawings of theatre buildings.

Det Kgl. Bibliotek – Aarhus

The Royal Danish Library – Aarhus

POSTAL ADDRESS
Victor Albecks Vej 1
DK–8000 Aarhus C

CONTACT
+45 89 46 20 22
kb@kb.dk

The home of the National Newspaper Collection and the National Media Collection (www.mediestream.dk). Aarhus University Library, Kasernen is the library and service centre for students and employees of the Department of Dramaturgy: library.au.dk/betjeningssteder/kasernen. All the material at the library can be sought for via library.au.dk.

The library receives plays from Aarhus Teater for the use of students of the Department of Dramaturgy and by individual request.

Theatre related material: monographs, periodicals, music, gramophone records, and radio/tv. Various materials can also be found in the Maps and Images Collection and the Handwritten Manuscript Collection. The Royal Danish Library – Aarhus also offers access to the National Media Collection's many digital compilations of radio, tv, music, film, and sound.

Det Kongelige Teaters Bibliotek og Arkiv

The Royal Theatre's Archives and Library

The Royal Theatre's Archives and Library has been closed. Its materials can now be found at the Danish National Archive (Rigsarkivet) and the Royal Danish Library respectively. A costume database can be found here: medie.kglteater.dk/dragtdatabase/login/welcome.jspx.

Det Kongelige Teaters Musikarkiv

Music Library, The Royal Danish Theatre

POSTAL ADDRESS
Postboks 2185
DK–1017 København K

ADGANG OPERAEN
Ekvipagemestervej 10
DK–1438 København K

CONTACT
+45 33 69 37 38
musikarkiv@kglteater.dk
www.kglteater.dk

Access is for the Royal Danish Theatre's personnel as well as by individual appointment. It has its own cataloguing system: title of the performance and, if appropriate, composer.

Established in approximately 1770, when the registering of musical scores for operas and ballets began. In the 1950s, the library was established as an independent department of the Royal Danish Theatre. The collections contain scores for operas, ballets and plays. Items are partly deposited at the Royal Danish Library (Music Collection).

Dokumentationscentralen for nordisk gruppeteater

The Documentation Center for Theatre-groups

POSTAL ADDRESS
Theatre and Performance Studies
Institute for Art and Cultural Studies
University of Copenhagen
Karen Blixens Vej 1
DK–2300 København S

The collection is in the basement archive. Enquiries to emeritus Stig Jarl stigjarl@hum.ku.dk.

The collection was established in 1974 on the initiative of then Professor Kela Kvam and thereafter run by a group of Theatre Studies students.

The collection includes, among other items, plays, photos, posters, sound recordings (reel-to-reel and cassette tapes) pertaining to Danish workers theatre between the wars and Danish group theatre from 1972 to 1980.

The collection also includes items pertaining to Swedish and Norwegian group theatre from 1972 to 1980, plus items regarding theatre and cultural policies pertaining to Denmark, Norway, and Sweden from the same period.

KADK Biblioteket for Arkitektur, Design, Konservering & Scenekunst

The KADK Library of Architecture, Design, Conservation, & Performing Arts

POSTAL ADDRESS
Danneskiold-Samsøes Allé 50
DK–1434 København K

CONTACT
+45 41 70 17 00
bibliotek@kadk.dk
kadk.dk/biblioteket

The National School of Performing Arts' library consists of four departments placed in Copenhagen, Odense, Fredericia, and Aarhus. The largest of the departments is part of the KADK library at Holmen, Copenhagen.

The Performing Arts Library assists the National School of Performing Arts' teaching and research. The collection primarily covers the following areas: plays, theatre history, dance, directing, scenography, choreography, stage productions and stage management, musicals, and performance.

The performing arts collection contains approximately 55,000 titles, of which 2,500 are play texts. In addition to this, the collection holds about 20 national and international periodicals on the performing arts as well as a collection of approximately 300 DVDs. You can search the collection via bib.kadk.dk

Københavns Museum

Museum of Copenhagen

POSTAL ADDRESS
Stormgade 20
DK–1555 København V

CONTACT
museum@kff.kk.dk
www.cphmuseum.kk.dk

Founded in 1901 with the objective of showing the history of Copenhagen and its development through the years. The museum is part of History and Art, Copenhagen Municipality.

The collection contains historical topographic images and items, including engravings, photos, programmes, and the like from the theatres of Copenhagen and various establishments of entertainment. For example, O. Chr. Hingsbergs Tivoliana collection of photos, scores, flyers, pamphlets etc. from approximately 1843 to 1929.

Nationalmuseet

National Museum of Denmark

POSTAL ADDRESS
Frederiksholms Kanal 12
DK–1220 København K

CONTACT
+45 33 13 44 11
post@natmus.dk
www.natmus.dk

The National Museum has several departments, many of which have their roots in the Royal Chamber of Danish Art, or the Old Nordic Museum. It is a national institution established in 1852 by royal decree.

Nationalmuseet, Forsknings- og Formidlingsafdelingen, Nyere Tid og Verdens Kulturer, Nyere Tids Samling

The National Museum, Research and Communication, Modern History and World Cultures, Collection of Modern History

Founded in 1855 by Bernhard Olsen with the aim of documenting the history of Danish culture from 1660 to today.

Costumes, objects, image archive plus a handwritten manuscript library and reading room are accessible by appointment. The lending of items is only available to museums and public institutions. Theatrical props, paintings, costumes, posters, and programmes are registered on card up to 1995. After this date, additional items have been registered digitally. Both archives are arranged after the principal of "factual registration".

The textile collection contains about 300 costumes, deposited by the Royal Danish Theatre. Some were originally privately owned costumes, while others are theatrical costumes registered with information about their size, material, colour, cut, sewing technique as well as theatrical historical information.

On December 31st 2011, the Theatre Museum at the Court Theatre ceased to be a nationally recognized museum. On behalf of the Royal Danish Library, the National Museum of Art, the National Library in Aarhus, and the National Museum, an assessment of the Theatre Museum's collection was carried out by The Modern History Collection. As a consequence of this, a number of items were transferred to the above-mentioned institutions.

The Circus Collection contains circus props and costumes, posters and programmes.

A collection of circus photographs and printed materials from Paul Neve, Frantz Olschansky and Frantz Jakielski. Copies of privately owned circus photos mounted on index cards.

Nationalmuseet, Musikmuseet – Musikhistorisk Museum og Carl Claudius' Samling

The Danish Music Museum – & The Carl Claudius Collection

FOR INDIVIDUAL VISITORS TO THE EXHIBITION AND VISITORS TO THE LIBRARY
Rosenørns Allé 22
DK–1970 Frederiksberg C

FOR GROUP VISITS, ADMINISTRATION PLUS POSTAL ADDRESS
Worsaaesvej 19, 2.
DK–1972 Frederiksberg C

CONTACT
musik@natmus.dk
www.natmus.dk/museerne/musikmuseet

The material in the museum's library and archive can be sought via the Music Museum's web-page: natmus.dk/museerne/musikmuseet/bibliotek-og-arkiv and www.bibliotek.dk.

The Music Museum's aim is to collect and preserve musical instruments and documentary material that shed light on music in a culture-historical context.

The collection contains musical instruments, books, pamphlets, musical scores, documents, RISM-books, RISM-scores, original art works, clippings, a small audio-visual collection, and items with relevance to the theatre. There is a permanent exhibition as well as special exhibitions.

Nordisk Teaterlaboratorium – Odin Teatret: Kuben – Forskning og Formidling

Nordisk Teaterlaboratorium – Odin Teatret: The Cube – Research and Dissemination

POSTAL ADDRESS
Særkærparken 144
DK–7500 Holstebro

CONTACT
+45 97 42 47 77
info@ntl.dk
www.ntl.dk

Nordisk Teaterlaboratorium – Odin Teatret was founded in Oslo in 1964 and moved to Holstebro in 1966. The archive covering the period from 1964–2018 has been donated to The Royal Danish Library. The theatre is still registering its activity and is experimenting with new archival formats that takes into consideration the process and the body of the actor.

Odense Bys Museer

Odense City Museums

POSTAL ADDRESS
Kulturarv
Overgade 48
DK–5000 Odense C

CONTACT
+45 65 51 46 01
museum@odense.dk
www.museum.odense.dk

The collections contain theatre-historical records, several objects as well as a large collection of portraits of actors/actresses with a connection to theatrical life on the island of Funen.

In addition, Mogens von Haven's ballet photographs.

Rigsarkivet

The Danish National Archives

READING ROOM
The Black Diamond
Søren Kierkegaards Plads 1
DK–1221 København K

CONTACT
mailbox@sa.dk
www.sa.dk

The Danish National Archive holds documents covering 450,000 meters of shelving, hereof approximately 280,000 meters in the Copenhagen department. Of theatre-historical items: the Royal Danish Theatre's archive from 1746 and on, the Royal Danish Chapels archive from 1784 and on, along with the documents that formerly were a part of the Royal Danish Theatre's Archive and Library. Furthermore, the archive contains items from various authorities within the administration of government. For example, the Danish Chancellery (–1848), Ministry of Finance (–1848), the Foundation ad Usos Publicos (1765–1842), Ministry of the Church and Education (1848–1916), Ministry of Education (1916–1961), Ministry of Justice (1848–1961), and the Ministry of Culture (1961–).

The private archives of several people connected to the Danish theatre are also to be found. Among others, J. H. S. Abrahams, August Bournonville, Harald Christensen, J. Chr. Hansen, A. W. Hauch, C. Hegermann-Lindencrone, Johan Ludvig Heiberg, Johanne Luise Heiberg, J. C. Normann, Th. Overskou, and Daniel Pilloy.

Provinsteatermuseet

The Museum of Theatres in the Provinces

POSTAL ADDRESS
Den Gamle By
DK–8000 Aarhus C

CONTACT
+45 86 12 31 88
mail@dengamleby.dk
www.dengamleby.dk

The collection contains – other than an actual theatre which was built in 1817 and relocated to Den Gamle By between 1956–1961 – five complete stage sets from Elsinore Theatre, proscenium curtain (1894) as well as parts of sets from the 1820s. Parts, prompter, and musical score archives from Elsinore Theatre 1793–1845, along with the Spierske Theatre Society and August Rasmussen's Society archives.

Letters and lesser documents pertaining to Danish theatre in the provinces. Posters and photos from theatres in the provinces. Posters from the Danish Royal Theatre from about 1835 to about 1870 (the collection is not complete). Stage management records, registers and costume designs from Aarhus Theatre and Casino in Copenhagen (Wantzin family). Stage photographs from Odense Theatre 1916–1946. 500 original drawings by Martin Hougaard for the newspaper "Demokraten" 1930–1956 approx. About 1000 original drawings by Asger Muchitsch for the newspaper "Aarhus Stiftstidende". Models of set designs, props etc., as well as objects pertaining to the running of cinemas and film.

Scenekunstarkiv.dk

Digital directory of the Danish theatres' repertoire from 2009/2010 and on. Replaces the ITI Year Book.

Statens Museum for Kunst

The Danish National Gallery

The Danish National Gallery no longer has a library open to the public. Most of its library has been transferred to the Royal Danish Library (see Denmark's Library of Art).

POSTAL ADDRESS
Statens Museum for Kunst
Den Kongelige Kobberstiksamling /
Department of Prints and Drawings
Sølvgade 48–50
DK–1307 København K

CONTACT
+45 33 74 84 94
smk@smk.dk
www.smk.dk/udforsk-kunsten/samlingerne/700-aars-kunst-og-kunsthistorie/om-kobberstiksamlingen/

STUDIESAL
+45 25 52 72 13
studiesal@smk.dk
www.smk.dk/besoeg-museet/praktisk-information/studiesalen

The collections contain Danish and foreign drawings (including water colours) and prints (engravings on wood, copper engravings, etchings, and lithographs plus variants of these techniques).

As far as items pertaining to the theatre are concerned, there are a limited number of drafts of set design and costumes, character portraits, portraits, architect drawings etc.

Storm – Museet for humor og satire

Storm – Museum of Humour and Satire

POSTAL ADDRESS
Frederiksberg Runddel
DK–2000 Frederiksberg

CONTACT
+45 38 10 20 45
info@frederiksbergmuseerne.dk
www.frederiksbergmuseerne.dk

Museum and archive pertaining to Danish entertainment theatre, that is to say, revue, operetta, cabaret, comedy, and stand-up comedy from the 1800s to today. The museum houses a revue historical archive that extensively looks at Danish revue from 1849 to today. Here one can find original scores to revue melodies, about 2000 records with old ballads, monologues, popular music, programmes, posters, photographs, and clippings with and about people with a connection to the world of revue. The museum has been amalgamated with the former Storm P. Museum.

Teatermuseet i Hofteatret

The Theatre Museum at The Court Theatre

POSTAL ADDRESS
Christiansborg Ridebane 10
DK–1218 København K

ENTRANCE TO THE MUSEUM
Christiansborg Ridebane 18
DK–1218 København K

CONTACT
+45 33 11 51 76
info@teatermuseet.dk
www.teatermuseet.dk

The museum documents the Danish theatre's development through 300 years through plays, directors' notes, scenographic models, costumes, costume drawings, shoes, props, make-up, personal records, books, interiors, lights, sound effect machines and other sound technology, tickets, programmes, posters, audience facilities, photos, gramophone records, DVDs, video and sound recordings, paintings, drawings, reviews, and all kinds of curiosities such as medals, furniture and more. Part of the collection was transferred to the Royal Danish Library, the National Museum of Art and the National Museum in 2011/2012.

Vejle Museerne

The Vejle Museums

POSTAL ADDRESS
Spinderigade 11E
DK–7100 Vejle

CONTACT
+45 76 81 31 00
museerne@vejle.dk
www.vejlemuseerne.dk

The Museum of Culture's collection contains, among other items, Alfred Jacobsen's puppet theatre from the 1940s with plays back from 1916, plus a puppet theatre from about 1907 marked "Prior" from Vilhelm Prior.

Vejle Stadsarkiv

Vejle City Archives

POSTAL ADDRESS
Vedelsgade 17
DK–7100 Vejle

CONTACT
+45 76 81 20 00
stadsarkivet@vejle.dk
www.arkiv.dk

The collection contains documents pertaining to Vejle Theatre, especially theatre and concert posters from 1834 to 1930. A directory of all the registered material pertaining to Vejle Theatre, which are deposited at the Vejle City Archives, can be found at www.arkiv.dk.

Items can be utilised in the reading room.

Aalborg Teater

Aalborg Theatre

POSTAL ADDRESS
Jernbanegade 11
DK–9000 Ålborg

CONTACT
+45 96 31 60 10
adm@aalborgteater.dk
www.aalborgteater.dk

The collection contains programmes from the theatre's performances since 1937. Part of the collection was lost during the German occupation during WWII. Items are ordered alphabetically and chronologically. The image archive has been transferred to the Local History Archive, which is in the process of digitising the theatres image archive. Exhibitions are held in the foyer of the theatre.

Aarhus Teater

Aarhus Theater

POSTAL ADDRESS
Teatergaden/Skolegade 9
DK–8000 Aarhus C

CONTACT
+45 89 33 23 00
+45 89 33 23 59
+45 28 77 22 52 (cell)
www.aarhusteater.dk
marianne.philipsen@aarhusteater.dk

Established in 1900 as A/S Aarhus Teater, Region and State financed.

Analogue documents

- Plays, promptbooks, character parts, and score sheets (1900–)
- Performance and character lists (1900–)
- Stage sets and costume department lists (1900–)
- Stage management and scene plans, scene and costume drawings, rehearsal and performance reports.
- Photos from performances, programmes, and posters (1900–)
- Documents, drawings, and records pertaining to the founding of the theatre (administration), and architecture (building works and re-building) as well as various receipts etc. (1898–)
- Photographs of the building, people, processes, workshops, events, etc. (1898–)
- Material concerning the old theatre in Arhus (1897–1900)

- Correspondance, copy books, business records and minutes, and contracts (1899–)
- Taped recordings of performances (1973–)
- Video and dvd recordings of performances (1980s–)
- Collection of books (theatre, cultural history, and fiction

University institutions within the areas of drama, performance, film, and theatre

Dramaturgi, ARTS

School of Communication and Culture Department of Dramaturgy and Musicology

POSTAL ADDRESS
Aarhus Universitet
Langelandsgade 139
DK–8000 Aarhus C

CONTACT
+45 87 16 12 00
au@au.dk
www.cc.au.dk

Film- og medievidenskab, Institut for Kommunikation

Film and Media Studies, Department of Communication

POSTAL ADDRESS
Det Humanistiske Fakultet
Københavns Universitet
Karen Blixens Plads 8
Bygning 16, 1. sal
DK–2300 København S

CONTACT
komm@hum.ku.dk
www.komm.ku.dk

Teater- og Performancestudier, Institut for Kunst- og Kulturvidenskab

Theatre and Performance Studies, Department of Arts and Cultural Studies

POSTAL ADDRESS
Københavns Universitet
Karen Blixens Vej 1
Bygning 16 + 21
DK–2300 København S

CONTACT
+45 35 32 81 99
studie_teater@hum.ku.dk
www.kunstogkulturvidenskab.ku.dk

Performance-design

POSTAL ADDRESS
Roskilde Universitet
Universitetsvej 1
Postboks 260
DK–4000 Roskilde

CONTACT
+45 46 74 20 00
ruc@ruc.dk
www.ruc.dk/performance-design-pa-roskilde-universitet

Nationally recognised Danish schools of education within the area of the performing arts

Den Danske Scenekunstskole

The Danish National School of Performing Arts

POSTAL ADDRESS
Den Danske Scenekunstskole
Per Knutzons Vej 5
DK–1437 København K

CONTACT
post@scenekunstskolen.dk
www.ddsks.dk

The Danish National School of Performing Arts was established on 1st January 2015 by amalgamating all the Danish state and state supported performing arts institutes of further education.

The following institutions were amalgamated into The Danish National School of Performing Arts: the School of Acting at Arhus Theatre, the School of Acting in Odense, the School of Playwrighting at Arhus Theatre, the Danish Musical Academy in Fredericia, Odsherred's School of Theatre, and the National Stage School.

Akademiet for utæmmet kreativitet

The Academy for untaimed creativity

POSTAL ADDRESS
Enghavevej 82B
DK–2450 København SV

CONTACT
afuk@afuk.dk
www.afuk.dk

The status of AFUK has changed throughout the years. A national circus artist education was about to be build (AFUK-AMoC), but has not been implemented yet. This is the rehearsal area for young circus artists.

The Faroe Islands

Illustration: Hamlet by Shakespeare. Performed by Hans Tórgard, Kjartan Hansen, Annika Johannessen, Sofía Nolsøe (large portrait), Egi Dam (small portrait). Director: Búi Dam. Set Designer: Sámal Blak, Det Ferösche Compagnie, The Nordic House and The National Theatre, 2019. Photographer: Finnur Justinussen.

It has not been possible to find an editor for this section. With the help of Gunnvá Zachariasen, Súni Joensen and Marita Dalsgaard the editor in chief, Anna Lawaetz, has collected names and addresses in order to give an overview to those interested in the theatre history of the Faroe Islands.

Landsbókasavnið

National Library of the Faroe Islands

POSTAL ADDRESS
J. C. Svabos gøta 16
Postboks 61
FO–110 Tórshavn

CONTACT
+298 340 525
lbs@landsbokasavnid.fo
www.landsbokasavnid.fo

Meginfelag Áhugaleikara Føroya

Amateur Theatre Association

POSTAL ADDRESS
Undir Pisuvarða 2
FO–100 Tórshavn

CONTACT
+298 285 624
maf@maf.fo
www.maf.fo

Tjóðpallur Føroya

The National Theatre

POSTAL ADDRESS
Tórsøgøta 9
FO–100 Tórshavn

CONTACT
+298 318 617
info@tjodpallur.fo
www.tjodpallur.fo

Tjóðsavnið

The Faroe Islands National Museum

POSTAL ADDRESS
Kúrdalsvegur 15
FO–188 Hoyvík

CONTACT
+298 340 500
savn@savn.fo
www.tjodsavnid.fo

Finland

Illustration: Seitsemän veljestä (Seven Brothers). Choreographer: Marjo Kuusela. The Finnish National Opera and Ballet, Helsinki, 1980. Photographer: Kari Hakli. The Finnish National Opera and Ballet.

FINNA

Online search service for Finland's archives, libraries, and museums

www.finna.fi

Finna.fi is an online search service where one can find material in Finnish archives, libraries, and museums. In addition to the national search service some content providers have their own Finna pages.

Helsingin kaupunginmuseo, esinekokoelmat

Helsinki City Museum

POSTAL ADDRESS
Box 4300
FI–00099 Helsingin Kaupunki

STREET ADDRESS
Aleksanterinkatu 16
FI–00170 Helsinki

CONTACT – ARCHIVES
Kati Selänniemi
+358 9 310 36476
kati.selanniemi@hel.fi
www.helsinginkaupunginmuseo.fi

The Archive is open by appointment only. Some of the material can be found in FINNA and can be used freely.

The museum's database is available in the museum's picture archive.

www.helsinginkaupunginmuseo.fi/kuvia-esineita-helsinkia/kuva-arkisto.

The largest collection of theatre material is the archive from the first theatre in Helsinki (Teaterhusaktiebolaget i Helsingfors). The collection contains records and other documents relating to building works and maintenance of the theatre 1825–1864, programme posters 1846–1859, and the theatre's location map from 1847. The collection also contains C. L. Engel's drafts of the façade of the building from 1826.

Also to be found are Helsinki City Theatre's programmes and posters 1968–2004, the Swedish Theatre's programmes from the 1890s to the 1950s, and marionettes etc. from Schmakoff's Marionette Theatre 1941.

Helsingin kaupunginteatteri

The Helsinki City Theatre

POSTAL ADDRESS
Ensi linja 2
FI–00530 Helsinki

CONTACT
+358 9 39401
www.hkt.fi/hktinenglish

The Helsinki City Theatre was founded in 1965 to replace the Helsinki People's Theatre and Worker's Theatre. The archive is available for researchers and other interested parties by appointment only.

The collections contain plays, programmes, photographs, newspaper clippings, posters, etc.

Kansalliskirjasto

The National Library of Finland

POSTAL ADDRESS
Post Box 15
FI–00014 University of Helsinki

STREET ADDRESS
Unioninkatu 36
FI–00170 Helsinki

CONTACT
+358 2941 23196
kk-palvelu@helsinki.fi
www.kansalliskirjasto.fi/en

The National Library was founded in 1640 and has, in principle, a complete collection of material published in Finland. Among them, theatre programmes and posters as well as material relating to the Russian theatre in Helsinki (the Alexander Theatre). In the manuscript collection, there are letters and documents relating to the theatre and people connected with it.

The National Library's collections can be found in the FINNA database here: kansalliskirjasto.finna.fi/?lng=en-gb.

Material from the National Library's scientific collection, national collection, and the music library's collection can be sought here.

The National Library has digitized newspapers which were published between 1771 and 1920. They are available to everyone and can be found here: digi.kansalliskirjasto.fi/etusivu?set_language=en.

Some more recent newspapers have also been digitized and are available online.

Doria www.doria.fi is a service where many universities and other organisations publish various digital material.

The web archive is a part of the national collection: verkkoarkisto.kansalliskirjasto.fi/va. The National Library stores domestic publications according to the law on the depositing and safekeeping of cultural material. Online material has been stored since 2006.

Kansallinen audiovisuaalinen instituutti

National Audiovisual Institute

POSTAL ADDRESS
Box 16
FI–00501 Helsinki

STREET ADDRESS
Sörnäisten rantatie 25 A
FI–00500 Helsinki

CONTACT
+358 295 338 000
kavi@kavi.fi
www.kavi.fi/en

The task of The National Audio-Visual Institute (KAVI) is to preserve film, tv, and radio programmes, to carry out research in the field, to carry out supervision over the provision of visual programmes, and to promote the understanding of the media.

The collection contains domestic and foreign full-length and short films, stills, plays, posters, etc. There is also a museum collection pertaining to film production and technique. There are regular film showings in the archive's own cinema, Kino Regina at the Central Library Oodi in Helsinki.

Kansallinen audiovisuaalinen instituutti / Kirjasto

National Audiovisual Institute / Library)

POSTAL ADDRESS
Box 16
FI–00501 Helsinki

STREET ADDRESS
Sörnäisten rantatie 25 A
FI–00500 Helsinki

CONTACT
+358 2 953 38006
kirjasto@kavi.fi
www.kavi.fi

The library of the National Audiovisual Institute is the country's largest information centre for the film industry; it is freely available to everyone. In the collection are books, sound recordings, journals, plays, and photographs. The institute's collection's database can be found here: kavi.verkkokirjasto.fi/en/etusivu.

At the library, it is possible to view the radio and tv archive's programme, the domestic film collection's digitized films, and the National Library's digital material.

Oulun yliopiston kirjasto

Oulu University Library

POSTAL ADDRESS
Box 7500
FI–90401 Oulun yliopisto

STREET ADDRESS
Linnanmaa
FI-Oulu

CONTACT
+358 294 483501
kirjasto@oulu.fi
www.oulu.fi/en/university/library
www.oulu.fi/en/university/library/contact-and-library-hours

The library was founded in 1959 and has received copies of printed material due to the legal deposit act since 1981. The library's collections can be searched here: oula.finna.fi.

The special collections here: libguides.oulu.fi/Erikoiskokoelmat.

Among the collections can be mentioned lecturer Ilkka Kaakinen's theatre collection consisting of photographs and mainly Finnish newspaper cuttings.

Sibeliusmuseums arkiv

Archive of the Sibelius Museum

POSTAL ADDRESS
Piispankatu 17
20500 Turku

CONTACT
+358 20 786 1476
sibmusarkiv@stiftelsenabo.fi
www.sibeliusmuseum.fi/en/sibeliusmuseum

The Sibelius Museum was founded in 1926 with the name "The Music Historical Collection at Åbo Akademi University". With Jean Sibelius' approval, the name was changed in 1949 to the Sibelius Museum.

Exhibition and conservation work is financed through funds from the privately run The Åbo Akademi University Foundation.

The Sibelius Museum's archive has material on domestic performing arts, especially opera and musical theatre in Finland. In the collection, one can find newspaper cuttings, concert programmes, posters, photographs, printed and handwritten sheet music as well as librettos. Among the institutions represented in the collection are The National Opera, Savonlinna Opera Festival, opera and theatre companies in Turku as well as opera and theatres in other parts of Finland (for example, Helsinki, Turku and Vaasa)

Parts of the collection can be found in the database Finna www.finna.fi, while other parts must be searched for manually via an older card index file. A large part of the collection has still, as yet, not been catalogued.

Sirkuksen ja tanssin tiedotuskeskus

Circus & Dance Info Finland

POSTAL ADDRESS
Tallberginkatu 1 C 93
FI–00180 Helsinki

CONTACT
info@circusdance.fi
circusdance.fi

Is an independent advisory organisation representing the circus and dance industries in Finland. The basic activities are funded by the Ministry of Education and Culture.

CDIF produces and disseminates information and statistics about the circus and dance sectors' activities and actors, conditions, results and impacts, and aim to develop these arts in our country. CDIF also facilitate international cooperation and exports in these fields.

CDIF maintains databases about dance and circus artists and performances in Finland, and a reference library in CDIF premises. CDIF also publishes annually a magazine in English, called Focus, focusing on circus and dance made in Finland.

A large part of the activities is carried out in the form of projects for which CDIF seeks separate private or public funding. CDIF cooperates on an ongoing basis with numerous Finnish and international organisations working in the performing arts, as well as with Finnish Cultural Institutes and Embassies around the world.

Circus & Dance Info Finland started its operations in 2023 as the earlier CircusInfo and Dance Info merged.

Svenska litteratursällskapet i Finland

Society of Swedish Literature in Finland

HELSINKI
Ritarikatu 5
Box 158
FI–00170 Helsinki

VAASA
Kauppapuistikko 23
FI–65100 Vaasa

CONTACT
+358 9 618 777
arkivet@sls.fi
www.sls.fi

The Society of Swedish Literature in Finland's archive is a rich source of information about Swedish speaking culture in Finland. In the archive can be found material regarding personal and literary history, theatre history, folk music and dance, folk culture and traditions, name traditions, language, and society. The material consists of everything from plays, drawings, and maps to photographs, sound, and film recordings, which the archive collects, handles, and mediates.

The theatre material in the collection comprises of plays, plays for individual parts, play catalogues, stage and costume sketches and drawings, posters, sheet music, song texts and sound recordings, advertisements, and videos of performances. The theatre archive also contains correspondence, protocols, company and yearly reports, contracts, financial ledgers, newspaper cuttings, reviews, and articles.

Among the collections with a connection to the theatre can be named the archives of the following theatres: Svenska Teatern, Lilla Teatern, Unga Teatern, Dramatiska Föreningen, Understödjs-föreningen för Svenska inhemska teatern, material connected to the Vasa Theatre, Folkteatern, Swedish domestic theatre, Svenska teaterföreningen i Finland, play manuscripts from the first half of the 1800s, etc.

Material relating to the theatre is also to be found in some personal and family archives. For example, in the archives of Vivica Bandler, Ester Margaret von Frenckell, Jutta and Benedict Zilliacus, Bengt Ahlfors, Monica Schildt, and Ralf Långbacka.

Material on summer theatre and amateur theatre can also be found.

Svenska Teaterns arkiv och bibliotek

Archives and Library of the Swedish Theatre

POSTAL ADDRESS
Svenska Teatern
Pohjoisesplanadi 2
FI–00130 Helsinki

CONTACT
+358 9 616 211
info@svenskateatern.fi
www.svenskateatern.fi

Suomalaisen Kirjallisuuden Seuran arkisto, kirjallisuuden ja kulttuurihistorian kokoelma

Finnish Literature Society, Collection of Literature and Cultural History

POSTAL ADDRESS
Box 259
FI–00171 Helsinki

STREET ADDRESS
Mariankatu 19 E
FI–00170 Helsinki

CONTACT
+358 201 131 262
arkisto@finlit.fi
www.finlit.fi

The Finnish Literature Society was founded in 1831. The collections contain, among other items, plays, letters, photographs, and a sound archive.

Suomen Näytelmäkirjailijat ja Käsikirjoittajat

Writers Guild of Finland

POSTAL ADDRESS
Agricolankatu 4 LH 46–48
FI–00530 Helsinki

CONTACT
+358 40 142 4527
info@sunklo.fi
www.sunklo.fi/en

The organisation was founded in 1921 by Finnish playwrights with the aim of promoting Finnish drama and protecting its members' interests. In the play bank www.naytelmat.fi one can find plays by both Finnish and foreign playwrights.

Suomen Kansallismuseo

The National Museum of Finland

POSTAL ADDRESS
Box 913
FI–00101 Helsinki

CONTACT
+358 295 33 6000
kansallismuseo@kansallismuseo.fi
www.kansallismuseo.fi

The general ethnographic collections are available to researchers, but the desired material must be ordered a few months in advance.

Material relating to the performing arts are two costumes from India as well as puppets and masks.

Suomen kansallisooppera ja -baletti

Finnish National Opera and Ballet

POSTAL ADDRESS
Box 176
FI–00251 Helsinki

STREET ADDRESS
Helsinginkatu 58
FI–00250 Helsinki

CONTACT
+358 9 4030 21
www.oopperabaletti.fi

INFORMATION SERVICES AND ARCHIVES
+358 40 5171446
marjaana.launonen@opera.fi

The National Opera was founded in 1911 and the Ballet in 1922.

The archive is available by appointment only and contains material relating to the administration of the National Opera and Ballet as well as opera and ballet performances. The material is divided into a document archive and a special collection. The document archive contains administrative documents such as records and correspondences. The special collection contains, among other things, programmes, press clippings, librettos, photographs, and video recordings. Parts of the collection have been digitized.

In the repertoire database Encore encore.opera.fi one can find data regarding opera and ballet performances since 1911.

Suomen Kansallisteatteri

The Finnish National Theatre

POSTAL ADDRESS
Läntinen Teatterikuja 1
FI–00100 Helsinki

CONTACT
+358 10 73311
tiedotus@kansallisteatteri.fi
www.kansallisteatteri.fi

ARCHIVIST LAURA SALONIEMI
+358 9 1733 1294
laura.saloniemi@kansallisteatteri.fi

The theatre archive was established in 1872 by Kaarlo and Emilie Bergbom. It is available by appointment only and contains domestic and foreign drama in Finnish, theatre literature, programmes, photographs, and documents about the history of Finland's National Theatre.

It has its own cataloguing system for plays.

Suomen valokuvataiteen museo

Finnish Museum of Photography

POSTAL ADDRESS
Tallberginkatu 1 G
FI–00180 Helsinki

CONTACT
+358 9 6866 3621
fmp@fmp.fi
www.valokuvataiteenmuseo.fi

The museum was founded in 1969 and is administered by The Finnish Museum of Photography. The photo service, library, and archive are available by appointment only: www.valokuvataiteenmuseo.fi/en/resources/image-service-library-archives.

There are 17 catalogued collections which contain photographs relating to the performing arts. Similar material can also be found in collections which have not been catalogued. A few local databases can be found in the museum's research room.

Freely available photographs can be found here: www.flickr.com/photos/valokuvataiteenmuseo.

Taideyliopiston kirjasto

The Uniarts Helsinki Library

The University of the Arts Library has three establishments: the campus library in Sörnäinen (The Academy of Art nd Theatre School). The campus library in Töölö (Sibelius-Akademin), and the library unit in Kuopio.

www.lib.uniarts.fi/en/general-info/opening-hours-and-contact

www.lib.uniarts.fi

The University of the Arts came into being via the merging of The Academy of the Arts, the Sibelius Academy, and the Theatre Academy in 2013. The library has functioned as the university's library from the beginning of 2017.

The library's physical collections offer a rich and comprehensive array of material within the field of the arts. A broad selection of journals, books and audio/visual material on art, music, and the performing arts is available as well as a large collection of sheet music, theatre programmes, along with special collections. The library also keeps copies of the students' written thesis. Manuscripts include Erkki Melartin's, Ernst Linko's, and Tauno Pylkkänen's compositions; as well as some of Jean Sibelius' manuscripts.

Material at the University of the Arts Library and the Arsca-database can be found via the search service FINNA: uniarts.finna.fi.

In addition, at the library, there are international databases for scientific articles, images, music, plays, opera, and much more.

Teatterimuseo

Theatre Museum

ADMINISTRATION
Kuortaneenkatu 3 C
FI–00520 Helsinki
teatterimuseo@teatterimuseo.fi
www.teatterimuseo.fi

INFORMATION SERVICE, ADDRESS FOR VISITORS
Kumpulantie 11
FI–00520 Helsinki
+358 40 1922 309
tietopalvelu@teatterimuseo.fi
www.teatterimuseo.fi/en/Collections

EXHIBITIONS, ADDRESS FOR VISITORS
Cable Factory
Tallberginkatu 1 G
FI–00180 Helsinki

EXHIBITION INFO
+358 40 1922 300
aula@teatterimuseo.fi
www.teatterimuseo.fi/en/Exhibitions

The Theatre Museum was founded in 1962 and it is the museum with national responsibility for the performing arts in Finland. The museum's collections contain material from the 1800s to the present day. The museum maintains a national collection of professional theatre, dance, opera, circus, and live art in Finland.

The museum's collections include costumes, scenographic models, as well as costume and scenographic sketches. The collection also includes puppets, technical equipment, as well as pieces of stage sets and props.

The Theatre Museum's archival collections include archives of both organisations and private individuals. The archives contain documents, photographs, and audio-visual material. In addition, there are separate collections of programmes, posters, and theatre reviews.

The Theatre Museum has carried out a survey of performing arts related materials in the collections of Finnish museums and archives. This information will eventually be published on the museum's website.

The museum's collections management system and a small reference library are available in the Research Room.

Teatterin tiedotuskeskus

Theatre Info Finland TINFO

POSTAL ADDRESS
Arkadiankatu 12 A 5
FI–00100 Helsinki

CONTACT
tinfo@tinfo.fi
www.tinfo.fi/en

Theatre Info Finland TINFO is an expert organization that works both nationally and internationally. TINFO produces theatre statistics, facilitates international mobility, and promotes Finnish performing arts and drama. The organization has an archive and a library, but its historical collections have been donated to the Theatre Museum.

The ILONA database at ilona.tinfo.fi contains information on professional theatre performances since the foundation of the first Finnish professional theatre in 1872. It is possible to search for data by performance, date, theatre, or author. The database is updated annually.

New Finnish plays are listed and presented in the New Plays from Finland database: www.tinfo.fi/fi/New-Plays-from-Finland.

The Drama translations database at www.tinfo.fi/en/Drama_translations_database contains information on translations of Finnish plays into other languages, as well as information on translators.

The Ensi-iltoja (Premieres) database www.tinfo.fi/fi/Ensi-iltoja contains information on productions at Finnish professional and amateur theatres since the year 2011 and onwards.

Information on touring performances can be found in the Touring Performances database at www.tinfo.fi/en/Touring_performances.

TINFO also produces Finnish theatre statistics annually that are freely accessible online at www.tinfo.fi/en/Theatre_Statistics, as well as TINFO News magazines available at www.tinfo.fi/en/TINFO-News-e-magazines. Newsletters in English are sent out to subscribers 2–3 times a year.

Turun kaupunginkirjasto

Turku Public Library

POSTAL ADDRESS
Linnankatu 2
FI–20100 Turku

CONTACT
+358 2 2620 624
kaupunginkirjasto@turku.fi
www.turku.fi/en/turku-city-library

The library was founded in 1863 and is partly a municipal library and partly a regional library with domestic collections. In the library's collections are sheet music, scores, CDs, sound tapes, slides, and microfilms.

In the special collection, Swedish drama from the 1600s, printed material, documents, and short plays published in the newspapers of the day can be found. Some of the material, among others play manuscripts, have been digitized and can be searched for here: vanha-kokoelma.kirjastot.fi/collections/show/2.

Työväen arkisto

The Labour Archives

POSTAL ADDRESS
Sörnäisten rantatie 25, 2. krs
FI–00500 Helsinki

CONTACT
+358 9 7743 110
info@tyark.fi
www.tyark.fi

The archive contains material relating to the theatre works of the Social Democratic workers organisation. For the main part, it deals with amateur theatre, but there is some material pertaining to professional theatre. The collection contains documents, photographs, posters, memorabilia, and interview material.

The theatre opened in 1860.The collections in the archive and library consist of theatre literature, play manuscripts, photographs, video tapes, programmes, posters, sheet music press clippings, administrative documents, as well as other material pertaining to the Swedish Theatre after 1975. In connection with the renovation of the theatre in 2012, archive material before 1975 was moved to the Society of Swedish Literature in Finland. The theatre's repertoire after 1945 is registered on a database. The theatre publishes the journal "Första raden" (Front Row), which has been published since 1995.

Turun yliopiston kirjasto

Turku University Library

POSTAL ADDRESS
Turku University Library
FI–20014 University of Turku

CONTACT
+358 29 450 2130
kirjasto@utu.fi
www.utu.fi/en/university/library

The library was founded in 1920 and duty copies include published books and journals from 1919.

The library has six units in Turku as well as units in Raisio and Rauma. The humanities, for the most part, are to be found in the Feeniks and Teutori libraries in Turku. An almost complete collection of published material connected with the theatre from 1919 and on is to be found at the Feeniks Library. Theatre publications before 1919, among others, play manuscripts from between 1857 to 1970 and radio plays from Radio Theatre are also to be found here. In addition, literature on opera and music biographies.

In the Teutori Library, material on the following can be found: theatre, dance, film, circus, performance, sound, music, art pedagogy, research in the arts and literature.

In the Newspaper and Ephemera Services in Raisio, an abundance of material relating to the performing arts can be found. In the collections, among others, are poster bills, brochures, and posters. Among the older material are poster bills from the Royal Circus from 1879.

The collection can be searched in the Volter database: utuvolter.fi/discovery/search?vid=358FIN_UTUR:VU1&lang=en.

The National Audio-Visual Institute's Ritva database with tv and radio programmes can be used at both the Feeniks and Teutori Library. In addition, there are other databases and electronic journals connected to the performing arts.

Åbo Akademis bibliotek

Åbo Akademi University Library

POSTAL ADDRESS
Tuomiokirkonkatu 2–4
FI–20500 Turku

CONTACT
+358 2 215 4180
biblioteket@abo.fi
www.abo.fi/en/library

Ålands landskapsarkiv

The Provincial Archives of Åland

POSTAL ADDRESS
Box 1060
AX–22111 Mariehamn

CONTACT
+358 18 25344
arkivet@regeringen.ax
www.arkivet.ax

In the Provincial Archives of Åland, archives of the Katrina Music Theatre and Theatre Society of Mariehamn can be found. The Katrina Music Theatre archive consists of mainly individual manuscripts and sheet music, but also other manuscripts and documents.

The Theatre Society of Mariehamn's archive consists mainly of manuscripts of performed plays from between 1914 and 2009.

Åbo Svenska Teater

The Swedish speaking theatre in Turku

POSTAL ADDRESS
Eerikinkatu 13
FI–20100 Turku

CONTACT
info@abosvenskateater.fi
www.abosvenskateater.fi/en/welcome

The archive material is not available to the general-public. Queries regarding the archive material can be sent to the theatre via email.

In Åbo Svenska Teater's small archive, the following, among other items, can be found: performance photos from the 1920s and on, theatre posters from the 1930s and on, programmes from the 1950s and on, plus scrapbooks, manuscripts, recent costume sketches, some old theatre backdrops, video and DVD recordings of performances, as well as documents and protocols.

Archive material about the Åbo Svenska Teater can also be found at the Document and Image unit at the Åbo Akademi University Library and the Theatre Museum's archive in Helsinki.

University institutions with courses in theatre, drama and/or film

Aalto-yliopisto

Aalto University

POSTAL ADDRESS
Box 11000
FI–00076 Aalto

CONTACT
+358 9 47001
kirjaamo@aalto.fi
www.aalto.fi/en

Helsingin yliopisto

University of Helsinki

POSTAL ADDRESS
Yliopistonkatu 3
Box 4
FI–00014 University of Helsinki

CONTACT
+358 2941 911
hy-arkki@helsinki.fi
www.helsinki.fi

Research in the arts

Jyväskylän yliopisto

University of Jyväskylä

POSTAL ADDRESS
Seminaarinkatu 15
Box 35
FI–40014 University of Jyväskylä

CONTACT
+358 1 4260 1211
kirjaamo@jyu.fi
www.jyu.fi

Department of music, art and culture studies

Oulun yliopisto

University of Oulu

POSTAL ADDRESS
Box 8000
FI–90014 University of Oulu

CONTACT
+358 2 9448 0000
oulun.yliopisto@oulu.fi
www.oulu.fi

ELOKUVATUTKIMUS / FILMFORSKNING / FILM STUDIES

KASVATUSTIETEIDEN TIEDEKUNTA, MUSIIKKIKASVATUKSEN TUTKINTO-OHJELMA / MUSIKPEDAGOGIK / MUSIC EDUCATION

FACULTY OF EDUCATION
Department of Educational Sciences and Teacher Education
Early Childhood Education
P. O. Box 2000
FI–90014 University of Oulu

Universities of the arts' and the Theatre Academy's educational and masters' courses

Taideyliopiston Teatterikorkeakoulu

Theatre Academy of Uniarts Helsinki

POSTAL ADDRESS
Box 20
FI–00097 Uniarts

CONTACT
+358 294 47 2000
teak.info@uniarts.fi
www.uniarts.fi/en/units/theatre-academy

Taideyliopiston Sibelius-Akatemia

The Sibelius Academy

POSTAL ADDRESS
Box 30
FI–00097 Uniarts

CONTACT
+358 294 47 2000
siba.info@uniarts.fi
www.uniarts.fi/en/units/sibelius-academy

Courses in opera

Tampereen yliopisto

Tampere University

POSTAL ADDRESS
Kalevantie 4
P. O. Box 1001
FI–33014 Tampere University

CONTACT
+358 294 5211
tau@tuni.fi
www.tuni.fi/en

Teatterityön Tutkinto-Ohjelma, Näty / Examensprogrammet i Teaterarbete / The Degree Programme in Theatre Arts
www.naty.uta.fi/?lang=en

The Centre for Practice as Research in Theatre T7 / Tutkivan Teatterityön Keskus T7 Päätalo
www.tuni.fi/en/research/centre-practice-research-theatre-t7

Turun yliopisto

University of Turku

POSTAL ADDRESS
FI–20014 University of Turku

CONTACT
+358 29 450 5000
kirjaamo@utu.fi
www.utu.fi

Institution for History, Culture and Research in the Arts
www.utu.fi/en/university/faculty-of-humanities/school-of-history-culture-and-arts-studies

Åbo akademi

Åbo Akademi University

POSTAL ADDRESS
Fabriksgatan 2
FI–20500 Åbo

CONTACT
+358 2 215 31
registrator@abo.fi
www.abo.fi

Greenland

Illustration: INUIT by Tuukkaq Teateret, 1978. Photographer: Unknown. Private collection.

Theatre Collections

At the moment, there is no single archive of theatre and the performing arts in Greenland. Other than privately owned items and documents as well as those in local museums in Greenland, and Greenlandic performances on YouTube, theatre items can be found in the following places:

Arktisk Institut

The Arctic Institute

POSTAL ADDRESS
Strandgade 102
DK–1401 København K

CONTACT
arktisk@arktisk.dk
www.arktiskinstitut.dk/en

Photo collection and ethnography including a photo collection of early amateur performances. Archive records concerning Greenland which are to be found in Greenland, Denmark or the Faeroe Islands can be accessed online via the home page of The Arctic Institute, Copenhagen.

Kalaallit Nunaata Radioa-T (KNR)

Greenlandic Broadcasting Corporation

POSTAL ADDRESS
KNR
Issortarfimmut 1
Box 1007
GL–3900 Nuuk

CONTACT
+299 36 15 00
info@knr.gl
www.knr.gl

YOUTUBE-PAGE
www.youtube.com/user/KNRgreenland

Radio plays since the 1950s, recorded theatre performances in Greenland's Radio and TV Archive

N.A.I.P/Nuummi Aliikkusersuisartut Isiginnaartitsisortullu Peqatigiit

Amateur Theatre Association in Nuuk

CONTACT
naipnuuk@gmail.com

FACEBOOK PAGE
www.prod.facebook.com/NAIP-Nuummi-171278836292947/about

Which has been active since 1959.

Nunatta Allagaateqarfia

Greenland's National Archive

POSTAL ADDRESS
Manutooq 1
P. O. Box 1090
GL–3905 Nuussuaq

CONTACT
+299 36 23 30
+299 32 34 79 (fax)
arkiv@arkiv.gl

NKA's digital collection including a photo collection can be accessed via da.nka.gl/digitale-samlinger/qangagooqgl.

Nunatta Atuagaateqarfia

National Library & Groenlandica

POSTAL ADDRESS
Manutooq 1
GL–3905 Nuussuaq

CONTACT
groenlandica@katak.gl
www.katak.gl/da/bibliotek/nationalbiblioteket

Nunatta Isiginnaartitsisarfia (NUIS)

The National Theatre of Greenland

POSTAL ADDRESS
Industrivej 27
Postboks 1627
GL–3905 Nuussuaq

CONTACT – ALLAFFEQARFIK
+299 38 13 70
+299 32 71 56 (fax)
info@nuis.gl
www.nuis.gl

Private archives (Hans Lynge, Villads Villadsen, Hans A. Hansen – crave permission), costume and photo collection, Nunatta Katersugaasivia Allagaateqarfialu (NKA) Greenland's National Museum & Archive.

NUIS-plays (since 2011) and documents from the Silamiut Theatre (since 1984).

Nunatta Katersugaasivia

National Museum

POSTAL ADDRESS
Hans Egedesvej 8
Boks 145
GL–3900 Nuuk

CONTACT
+299 32 26 11
nka@natmus.gl
www.nka.gl

Tuukkaq Theatre (since 1975), Fjaltring, Lemvig – private archive

POSTAL ADDRESS
Tuukkaq Teateret
v/Reidar Nilsson and Erninguaq Poulsen
Rubyvej 38
Fjaltring
DK–7620 Lemvig

Iceland

Illustration: Fósturmold by Guðmundur Steinsson. Performed by Jóhann Pálsson, Erlingur Gíslason and Guðjón Ingi Sigurðsson. Director: Kristbjörg Kjeld. Set Designer: Jón Gunnar Árnason, Tjarnarbær, Reykjavík, 1965. Photographer: unknown. Collection: LMÍ 2022/2 Jóhann Pálsson, Theatre Museum, National and University Library of Iceland.

Bandalag íslenskra leikfélaga

Coalition of Icelandic Theatre Companies

POSTAL ADDRESS
Kleppsmýrarvegur 8
IS–104 Reykjavík

CONTACT
+354 551 6974
info@leiklist.is
www.leiklist.is

The Coalition of Icelandic Theatre Companies is an association of amateur theatres in Iceland. The association has a service centre where one can find a collection of playscripts. The collection's focus is to acquire and maintain plays that are written in Icelandic or have been translated into Icelandic. The collection is the only drama library in Iceland operating nationally and serving everyone who seeks plays be they theatres, theatre groups, schools, colleges, or kindergartens, and for those who are studying literature or drama at universities. There are now about 4000 plays at the museum and the majority of them are also preserved electronically. The association runs a webpage, leiklist.is, where information about the library's plays is accessible for all.

Borgarskjalasafn Reykjavíkur

The Reykjavik Municipal Archives

POSTAL ADDRESS
Tryggvagata 15
IS–101 Reykjavik

CONTACT
+354 411 6060
borgarskjalasafn@reykjavik.is
www.borgarskjalasafn.is

The Reykjavik Municipal Archives maintains documents pertaining to theatre groups in Reykjavik. Among others, the Reykjavik City Theatre and Perlan, a theatre group for the disabled and for UNIMA in Iceland. Parts of the Reykjavik Theatre Company's archive can be found on the Municipal Archive's webpage.

Landsbókasafn Íslands – Háskólabókasafn – Leikminjasafn Íslands

National and University Library of Iceland – Theatre Museum of Iceland

POSTAL ADDRESS
Arngrímsgata 3
IS–107 Reykjavík

CONTACT
+354 525 5673
leikminjasafn@landsbokasafn.is
sigridur.jonsdottir@landsbokasafn.is
www.landsbokasafn.is
www.leikminjasafn.is

The National and University Library of Iceland has a large collection of plays, theatre programmes, books, and other printed items related to the performing arts. Since 2019, the library has been responsible for running the Icelandic Theatre Museum. The aim of the museum is to catalogue items pertaining to the history of Icelandic theatre and to hold exhibitions. The museum collects, maintains, catalogues, studies, and exhibits historical theatre material, and any form of data concerning theatre, performing arts, theatres, and theatre groups, both professional and amateur. The museum also manages the classification and the archiving of private collections from Icelandic theatre professionals that contain books, plays, posters, drawings, photographs, etc. The database on the Theatre Museum's webpage contains information about theatre performances in Iceland from the start of the 1900s to today. A large collection of recordings and videos of performances is in the process of being digitized and made available to the public.

Listaháskóli Íslands

Iceland University of the Arts

POSTAL ADDRESS
Þverholt 11
IS–105 Reykjavík

CONTACT
+354 545 2200
lhi@lhi.is
www.lhi.is

Iceland University of the Arts is an institution for further education connected to, among others, the performing arts. The university's library is a modern research facility within the fields of painting, architecture and design, the performing arts and music. Plays are stored as well as recordings of drama students' performances.

Þjóðminjasafnið

The National Museum of Iceland

POSTAL ADDRESS
Suðurgata 41
IS–101 Reykjavík

CONTACT
+354 530 2200
thjodminjasafn@thjodminjasafn.is
www.thjodminjasafn.is

The National Museum of Iceland is the centre of Iceland's cultural heritage and research into items of historical cultural significance. The museum presents the cultural heritage of Icelanders from their very beginnings to this day. The National Museum has entered into an agreement with the Theatre Museum of Iceland to keep and store three dimensional performing arts objects. Historical theatre items that are held at the National Museum are, among others, tied to the painter and visionary Sigurdur Gudmundsson, his set design and drawings. The museum also has historical theatre photographs that are kept at the Icelandic Museum of Photography.

Þjóðleikhúsið

The National Theatre of Iceland

POSTAL ADDRESS
Hverfisgata 19
IS–101 Reykjavík

CONTACT
+354 585 1200
leikhusid@leikhusid.is
www.leikhusid.is

Iceland's National Theatre stores a multitude of resources from its establishment in 1950 to today. This includes all manuscripts and programmes of plays that have been performed. Photographs and some designs are available of performances and are kept at the Icelandic Museum of Photography at the National Museum.

RÚV – Ríkisútvarpið

The Icelandic National Broadcasting Service

POSTAL ADDRESS
Efstaleiti 1
IS–150 Reykjavík

CONTACT
+354 515 3000
safn@ruv.is
www.ruv.is

In accordance with a law from 2013, RÚV (The Icelandic National Broadcasting Service) stores sound recordings, films and theatre recordings, and various other material that can be of cultural and historical significance for the Icelandic nation. The role of the archive is to maintain programmes and make them available for future programming and research. RÚV's archives are open and accessible to the public on weekdays from 12pm to 4pm. Requests can be sent to safn@ruv.is.

Norway

Illustration: Reisen til julestjernen (The Journey to the Star of Bethlehem), The National Theatre, Oslo, 1924. The National Library of Norway.

Aust-Agder museum og arkiv

Aust-Agder Museum and Archives

POSTAL ADDRESS
Avd. KUBEN
Parkveien 16
NO–4838 Arendal

CONTACT
+47 37 01 79 00
postmottak@aama.no
www.kubenarendal.no

Theatre archive from Arendal Drama Association ADS. Archival material from the beginning in 1796 and on: management protocols, scrapbooks, inventory, correspondence, cast lists, accounts, performed plays and more.

Bergen Offentlige Bibliotek

Bergen Public Library

POSTAL ADDRESS
Strømgaten 6
NO–5015 Bergen

CONTACT
+47 55 56 85 00
post@bergenbibliotek.no
www.bergenbibliotek.no

Norway's second biggest public library, established in 1872. Documents linked to Ole Bull and Henrik Ibsen, relating to their time at Det norske Theater. Also the world's biggest Edvard Grieg Collection as donated by his widow Nina Grieg in 1927. The music collection also contains material concerning composers Harald Sæverud and Sverre Bergh.

Det Norske Teatret

The Norwegian Theatre

POSTAL ADDRESS
Kristian IV's gaten 8
NO–0164 Oslo

CONTACT
+47 22 47 38 00
hei@detnorsketeatret.no
www.detnorsketeatret.no

One of Norway's foremost institutional theatres, established 1913. Most of the archive has been transferred to the National Library of Norway, such as photographs and scripts. The theatre performs plays and musicals in Nynorsk, a Norwegian without Danish traces, but rather from rural Norwegian dialects.

Drammens Museum for kunst og kulturhistorie

The Drammen Museum for Art and Cultural History

POSTAL ADDRESS
Konnerudgata 7
NO–3045 Drammen

CONTACT
+47 32 20 09 30
post@drammens.museum.no
www.drammens.museum.no

The collection includes documents concerning The Drama Association and theatre productions at Drammen 1782–1853: Deeds, bonds, share certificates, manuscripts of prologues, songs for special occasions, letters, management protocols, some programmes and posters, account reports etc.

Frederikshalds Teater

Frederikshald Theatre

POSTAL ADDRESS
Østfold Museum
Halden Historical Collection
Teatergata 3
NO–1776 Halden

CONTACT
+47 69 11 56 50
hhs@ostfoldmuseene.no
www.ostfoldmuseene.no/avdelingene/halden-historiske-samlinger/fredrikshalds-teater-2

Established in 1838 on the initiative of The Drama Association.

Henrik Ibsen Museum

The Henrik Ibsen Museum (Telemark Museum)

POSTAL ADDRESS
Telemark Museum
Venstøphøgda 74
NO–3721 Skien

CONTACT
+47 35 54 45 00
post@telemark.museum.no
www.telemarkmuseum.no/henrik-ibsen-museum

Ibsen's childhood home in the country outside Skien.Venstøp Farm was a gift to Telemark Museum from the Løvenskiold family, and opened in 1958. Open May-August. Exhibitions with original material from Henrik Ibsen's childhood and educational material.

Ibsen-muséet

The Ibsen Museum in Grimstad

POSTAL ADDRESS
Grimstad Town Museum
Henrik Ibsens Gate 14
NO–4878 Grimstad

CONTACT
+47 37 04 04 90
post@gbm.no
www.gbn.no/ibsenmuseet

The museum is the country's oldest of its kind and opened in 1916. The museum is housed in the building where Henrik Ibsen worked as a pharmacist's assistant in the years 1847–1850, and where he wrote his first play Catiline. The collection includes clothes and objects that belonged to Henrik Ibsen as well as original manuscripts.

Ibsenmuséet

The Ibsen Museum (The Norwegian Folk Museum)

POSTAL ADDRESS
Norsk Folkemuseum
Henrik Ibsens Gate 26
NO–0255 Oslo

CONTACT
+47 40 02 36 30
ibsen@norskfolkemuseum.no
www.ibsenmuseet.no

The home of Henrik Ibsen for the last 11 years of his life. Fully restored writer's home with original interior and decor. The library holds Henrik and Suzannah Ibsen's book collection, as well as his Medals of Merit from Norway and abroad.

Kirsten Flagstad Museum

The Kirsten Flagstad Museum (Anno Museum)

POSTAL ADDRESS
Anno Museum
Kirkegaten 11
NO–2318 Hamar

CONTACT
+47 62 54 27 00
post@kirsten-flagstad.no
www.kirsten-flagstad.no

A private collection regarding opera singer, Wagnerian soprano and first head of The Norwegian National Opera, Kirsten Flagstad (1895–1962). Her costumes are spectacular and include several examples on loan from the Metropolitan Opera Archives.

Nasjonalbiblioteket

The National Library of Norway

POSTAL ADDRESS
Henrik Ibsens gate 110
NO–0255 Oslo

CONTACT
+47 81 00 13 00
veiledningen@nb.no
spesiallesesalen@nb.no
bilder@nb.no
musikk@nb.no
film@nb.no
www.nb.no

With archives regarding all facets of Norwegian history, The National Library is one of Norway's foremost culture institutions, with unique collections of plays, special collections of books, music, radio and TV programmes, film, theatre, maps, posters, pictures, photographs, electronic documents and newspapers.

Since 1813, the University of Oslo Library had functioned as both a library for the university and a national library. In 1989, Norway established a repository in Rana in the northern part of the country as part of the national library, with a mandate to preserve everything published within the country in compliance with a revised version of the Legal Deposition Act.

The National Library of Norway started a digitization process in 2006 with a goal to digitize its entire collection. Today, The National Library of Norway is essentially a digital library. For access outside Norwegian IP-space, users have to apply through special form, or, contact the Special Reading Room to study plays, posters, theatre programs and letters. Music collection with scores, stage and opera music. Film and broadcasting section with its own viewing room and archives after most authors and theatres. The National Library holds the world's biggest Henrik Ibsen collection, with all his manuscripts and letters available at nb.no.

Nationaltheatret

The National Theatre (Oslo)

POSTAL ADDRESS
Johanne Dybwads plass 1
NO–0161 Oslo

CONTACT
+47 22 00 14 00
resepsjon@nationaltheatret.no
www.nationaltheatret.no

Norway's most prominent venue for performing arts, established in 1899 with Bjørn Bjørnson as its first director.

The main part of its archive has been transferred to the National Library of Norway. A digital performance database with information on former productions, with historical photographs, can be found at forest.nationaltheatret.no.

Norsk Revyfaglig Senter

The Norwegian Revue Centre

POSTAL ADDRESS
Norsk Revyfestival
Bygdatunet
NO–7977 Høylandet

CONTACT
+47 74 32 10 50
festival@revy.no
www.revy.no

Founded in 1990. Large script bank with revue texts in the History of Norwegian Revue Archive. Works in cooperation with Sweden and Denmark.

RAS Regional Arena for Samtidsdans

The Regional Arena for Contemporary Dance (Sandnes)

POSTAL ADDRESS
Sandnes kulturhus
Mauritz Kartevolds plass 1
NO–4306 Sandnes

CONTACT
+47 51 60 20 00
adm@sandnes-kulturhus.no
www.sandnes-kulturhus.no/ras-dans

RAS is a project program for contemporary dance. The program consists of local, Norwegian and international representation of the art of dance. RAS offers recidencies for international dancers and choreographers, with consecutive application deadline. Digital archive since 2014.

Riksteatret

The National Norwegian Touring Theatre

POSTAL ADDRESS
Gullhaug Torg 2
NO–0484 Oslo

CONTACT
+47 24 14 42 00
arkiv@riksteatret.no
www.riksteatret.no

Riksteatret was established by law in 1948. Its first performance was in Kirkenes in 1949, with Sigurd Christiansen's play *En reise i natten*. The theatre plays on about 200 different stages throughout the country. Riksteatret keeps their own archive at their premises in Nydalen, Oslo.

Ringve Musikkmuseum

Ringve Music Museum

POSTAL ADDRESS
MiST Museene i Sør-Trøndelag
Lade allé 60
NO–7041 Trondheim

CONTACT
+47 73 87 02 80
post@ringve.no
www.ringve.no

The Ringve collection includes, among other things, musical instruments, musical items, and original manuscripts. A large photography collection with Norwegian musicians and composers, and sound archive with many kinds of recording systems represented. In addition, an archive with people and institutions from the national and local music scene. Library with books about music and cultural history.

Rogaland Teater

Rogaland Theatre (Stavanger)

POSTAL ADDRESS
Teaterveien 1
NO–4005 Stavanger

CONTACT
+47 51 91 90 00
post@rogaland-teater.no
www.rogaland-teater.no

Rogaland Teater holds its own archive with posters, theatre programmes and scripts. Established 1947.

Sceneweb

Sceneweb (A National Performing Arts Archive)

POSTAL ADDRESS
Dance and Theatre Centre
Observatoriegata 1b
NO–0254 Oslo

CONTACT
+47 23 10 09 80
redaksjon@sceneweb.no
www.sceneweb.no

Digital performing arts database for professional performing arts. Search for drama titles, performers' names, dance groups, institutions, venues and more. Photo gallery with photographs and posters, many of them for downloading.

Senter for Ibsen-studiers bibliotek

UiO – Centre for Ibsen Studies, Faculty of Humanities, University of Oslo

POSTAL ADDRESS
Henrik Wergelands hus
Niels Henrik Abels vei 36
NO–0313 Oslo

CONTACT
+47 22 85 80 19
kristin.kosberg@ibsen.uio.no
www.hf.uio.no/is/tjenester/Ibsen-biblioteket

The library at the Centre for Ibsen Studies is a research library that covers the subject area of Ibsen Studies. It is open for everyone.

Statsarkivet i Kristiansand

The Regional State Archives in Kristiansand

POSTAL ADDRESS
Märthas vei 1
NO–4633 Kristiansand

CONTACT
+47 48 05 56 66
post@arkivverket.no
www.arkivverket.no/om-oss/besok-oss/statsarkivet-i-kristiansand

The collection includes archive material pertaining the Christiansand's Drama Association, founded in 1787. Statsarkivet i Kristiansand has its own reading room and digitalizes archival material on demand.

Statsarkivet i Trondheim

The Regional State Archives in Trondheim

POSTAL ADDRESS
Maskinistgata 1
NO–7042 Trondheim

CONTACT
+47 48 05 56 66
post@arkivverket.no
www.arkivverket.no/om-oss/besok-oss/statsarkivet-i-trondheim

The collection includes documents concerning theatrical activity in Trondheim in the 1800s, among others, Gustav Wilhelm Selmer and The United Drama Association in Trondheim. The library has 60 seats, a reading room, and research rooms.

Statsarkivet i Stavanger

The Regional State Archives in Stavanger

POSTAL ADDRESS
Richard Johnsensgate 12
NO–4021 Stavanger

CONTACT
+47 48 05 56 66
post@arkivverket.no
www.arkivverket.no/om-oss/besok-oss/statsarkivet-i-stavanger

Archival material from Stavanger Faste Scenee (1914–1921), Stavanger Drama Association (1923–1929), Stavanger Theatre (1883–1913, 1921–1926), and Rogaland Theatre (1947–) Library with over 10 000 titles. Own reading room.

Teaterarkivet

The Theatre Archives, University of Bergen

POSTAL ADDRESS
Department of Linguistic, Literary, and Aesthetic Studies
University of Bergen
Sydnesplassen 7
NO–5020 Bergen

CONTACT
+47 55 58 24 00
post@lle.uib.no
www.uib.no/lle/24801/teaterarkivet

Theatre collection with theatre programmes, posters, correspondence, scores, plays, pictures, scenography sketches and costume drawings from The Drama Association in Bergen (1794–), The Norwegian Theatre in Bergen (1850–1863), The National Theatre (1876–), and The Theatre of Comedy in Bergen (1933–1964). Some material on amateur theatres and school theatre.

Teatermuseet

The Theatre Museum (Oslo Museum)

POSTAL ADDRESS
Oslo Museum
Frognerveien 67
NO–0266 Oslo

CONTACT
+47 23 28 41 90
post@oslomuseum.no
www.oslomuseum.no/teatermuseet

The Theatre Museum in Oslo opened in 1939 and from 2010 co-located with the Oslo Museum in Frognerparken. The Theatre Museum has a large collection of costumes from, among others, Christiania Theatre, The National Theatre, The Norwegian Theatre, The Central Theatre (Centralteatret), The New Theatre (Det Nye Teater), and The Norwegian Opera and Ballet. A large collection of costumes from Rita Tori, Love Krohn, and the New Norwegian Ballet. The collection contains paintings, drawings, photographs, props, furniture, and approximately 100 scenography models.

See oslobilder.no for many photographs from the Theatre Museum.

Teatersamlingen

The Theatre Collection, University Museum of Bergen

POSTAL ADDRESS
University Museum of Bergen, art and culture history collections
Haakon Sheteligs plass 10
NO–5007 Bergen

CONTACT
+47 55 58 31 24
post@um.uib.no
www.uib.no/universitetsmuseet/63810/teatersamlingen

The collection consists of items and objects connected to theatre activities in Bergen going back to the early 1800s: Costumes, masks, props, stage sets, paintings, models and more. Open for scholarly researchers and the public.

Teatersamlingen

The Theatre Collection, NTNU University Library (Trondheim)

POSTAL ADDRESS
NTNU University Library Special Collections
Gunnerusbiblioteket Kalvskinnsgt. 1B
NO–7491 Trondheim

CONTACT
+47 91 89 78 59
spesialsamlingene@ub.ntnu.no
www.ntnu.no/ub/spesialsamlinger/teatersamlinger

Large theatre collection dating back to the 1700s. Archive from Throndhjem's Theatre, Trondheim National Stage, and Trøndelag Teater. Repertoire lists, cast photos, posters, programmes, and an almost complete collection of physical and digital plays. Theatre models are housed in the Dora Library at the Archive Centre, Maskinist Gate 1.

University institutions and academies with courses in theatre, drama and/or film

Drama og teater

Drama and Theatre, NTNU University of Trondheim

POSTAL ADDRESS
Institute of Art and Media Studies
Norwegian University of Science and Technology
Edvard Bulls veg 1
NTNU Dragvoll
NO–7491 Trondheim

CONTACT
+47 73 59 18 20
kontakt@ikm.ntnu.no
www.ntnu.no/ikm

The Institute of Art and Media Studies (IKM) houses both a practical-aesthetic and an academic education. Courses in drama and theatre, film studies, film and video production, media studies, and art history.

Teatervitenskap

Theatre Studies, University of Bergen

POSTAL ADDRESS
Institute of Theatre Studies
University of Bergen
Sydnesplassen 7
NO–5020 Bergen

CONTACT
+47 55 58 24 00
post@lle.uib.no
www.uib.no/fag/teatervitenskap

Courses at bachelor and master's level. Special areas of research are Norwegian theatre history, the reception of Ibsen's plays in Norwegian theatres, postmodern theatre theory, performance analysis, and theatre criticism.

Teaterhøgskolen

The Academy of Theatre

POSTAL ADDRESS
KHiO Oslo National Academy of the Arts
Kunsthøgskolen i Oslo
Fossveien 24
NO–0551 Oslo

CONTACT
+47 22 99 55 00
postmottak@khio.no
www.khio.no/studier.teaterhogskolen

Since it was established in 1953, the Academy of Theatre has been Norway's leading educational institution for the acting professions. The Academy offers a three-year Bachelor's course for actors and directors and a two-year Master's course in theatre, specialising in acting, direction, stage writing and stage design. The department also offers a practice-oriented teacher training course (PPU) for drama teachers.

The Academy embraces both traditional and experimental techniques.

Senter for Ibsen-studier

Centre for Ibsen Studies – University of Oslo

POSTAL ADDRESS
Faculty of Humanities
Henrik Wegelands hus
Niels Henrik Abels vei 36
NO–0313 Oslo

CONTACT
+47 22 85 50 50
hf-studieinfo@hf.uio.no
www.hf.uio.no/is

The Centre offers a two year Master programme in Ibsen Studies, and a number of Bachelor courses. The Centre for Ibsen Studies is a national and international hub for research, documentation, and teaching within the field of Henrik Ibsen's authorship and interpretation of his works. The Annual Ibsen Lecture series showcases major international figures who have engaged with Ibsen and his works from various perspectives.

Sweden

Illustration: Unidentified woman, unknown year and photographer. Glass negative, the Music- and Theatre Library of Sweden.

Arena Theatre Institute

POSTAL ADDRESS
Sandövägen 59
Norrnäs
SE–139 50 Värmdö

CONTACT
+46 8 570 240 40
arena.per@swipnet.se

The museum's collection consists of the Arena Theatre Boat, built in 1968. The Foundation also has two other theatres at the same address: a circus arena located outdoors, and a demonstration room called The Model, which can be used to show different types of theatre stages.

The Swedish Theatre's Technical Collection consists of historical spotlights and other theatrical technical equipment.

There is also a play library with both published and unpublished material, as well as a collection of books, archive material and drawings of theatre venues from around the world.

Birgit Nilsson museum

Birgit Nilsson Museum

POSTAL ADDRESS
Birgit Nilssons väg 27
Svenstad
SE–269 91 Båstad

CONTACT
+46 43 131 18 60
info@birgitnilsson.com
www.birgitnilsson.com

Carina Ari biblioteket

The Carina Ari Library

POSTAL ADDRESS
Box 6064
SE–102 31 Stockholm

CONTACT
+46 8 662 65 70
biblioteket@carina.se
www.carinaari.se/library_sv.html

The library was founded in 1969 via a donation from the dancer and choreographer Carina Ari. It is a research library with books on dance in all its various forms from around the world. In addition, most dance journals can be found here. The collection is quite complete regarding what was published on dance before 1850 and well equipped with newer works.

Searching the catalogue can be done here: carinaari.se/sv/research.

There is also a large collection of videos of dance performances. Many of the dance performances that took place at Dansens Hus (The Dance House) in Stockholm are documented on video. The library also invites all choreographers and dancers who so wish to have their performances videoed so they can become a part of the library's archive.

Cirkusakademien

The Circus Academy

POSTAL ADDRESS
Stopvägen 123
SE–188 36 Bromma

CONTACT
cirkusakademien@gmail.com
www.cirkusakademien.se

The Academy for the Preservation of the Art of the Circus was founded in 1973 with the aim of promoting the circus as a recognized art form. The Circus Academy has an archive, runs a museum in southern Sweden, and publishes the journal Cirkulara Notiser (Circular Notices).

The collection includes photographs, posters, programmes, and cuttings and objects related to circus artists, circuses, and variety artists: Maria Adolfi, Rune Zetterlund, Dolf Schreiber, Bengt Alvo-Johansson, Trolle Rhodin sr., Folkeparkens Artistförmedling, China-Variety, and Harald Grannwing.

In addition, there is a library with books, journals, and scrapbooks as well as videotapes of circus and variety artists at work.

Sveriges cirkusmuseum

The Swedish Circus Museum

POSTAL ADDRESS
Skolan
Ingelsträde
SE–263 91 Höganäs

CONTACT
+46 704 614 783
www.cirkusmuseum.net

Dansmuseet

The Dance Museum

POSTAL ADDRESS
Box 7213
SE–103 68 Stockholm

CONTACT
+46 8 441 76 51
erik.mattsson@dansmuseet.se
www.dansmuseet.se

The museum has its origins in Les Archives Internationales de la Danse, which the Swedish art collector and leader of the Swedish Ballet, Rolf de Maré, opened in Paris in 1933. The museum was founded by Rolf de Maré in 1953. It has a collection of costumes, pictures, and objects related to dance from all over the world. There are also archives, a library, and a video collection of dance in all its forms from all around the world. Some well-known archives are, among others, The Swedish Ballet, Birgit Cullberg, and Kurt Jooss.

Dramatikerförbundet

The Writers' Guild of Sweden

POSTAL ADDRESS
Drottninggatan 85
SE–111 60 Stockholm

CONTACT
+46 8 21 33 10
info@dramatiker.se
www.dramatiker.se

The Writers' Guild was founded in 1941 and is an interest organisation that organizes screenwriters, playwrights, and translators of drama. The Guild administers two scholarships that are awarded to people active in the Guild's professional groups: Henning Mankell's and Lars Molins Scholarship respectively.

DramaDirekt

POSTAL ADDRESS
c/o Dramatikerförbundet
Drottninggatan 85
SE–111 60 Stockholm

CONTACT
+46 8 402 36 44
info@dramadirekt.se
www.dramadirekt.se

DramaDirekt is a play bank run by the Writers' Guild of Sweden with the financial support of the Swedish Council of Culture. It was established in 1997 and seeks, as its main task, to promote, disseminate, and make available written drama in Sweden and abroad. The plays in the database can be bought both by theatre professionals and private individuals.

Plays can be searched for here: www.dramadirekt.se/?s=. They can be bought both in printed and digital form

Figur- och dockteatercentrum

The Centre of Puppetry

POSTAL ADDRESS
Kulturhuset
Valthornsgatan 13
Box 73
SE–421 21 Västra Frölunda

CONTACT
+46 31 366 27 20
torbjorn.alstrom@afh.goteborg.se
www.goteborg.se/wps/portal?uri=
gbglnk %3a20161016122630935

The Centre of Puppetry's main aim is to spread knowledge about the world of puppets and puppet theatre. There is a library with books about puppet theatre. In addition, there is a puppet workshop as well as exhibitions that illuminate puppet theatre from around the world.

Göteborgs stadsarkiv med Folkrörelsernas arkiv

Gothenburg's city archives with the People's Movements archive

Look for Regionarkivet, Västra Götalandsregionen och Göteborgs stadsmuseum.

Göteborgs stadsmuseum

Museum of Gothenburg

POSTAL ADDRESS
Norra Hamngatan 12
SE–411 14 Göteborg

CONTACT
+46 31 368 36 00
stadsmuseum@kultur.goteborg.se
www.goteborgsstadsmuseum.se

THE THEATRE COLLECTIONS

The former Theatre History Museum was founded by the Theatre Historical Society and was inaugurated in 1954 at the Lorensberg Theatre. The museum and its collection were handed over to the city of Gothenburg in 1967. In 1995, the museum was incorporated into the Museum of Gothenburg and the collection was transferred to the East India House where they are a section of the Museum of the city. The Museum of Gothenburg belongs to the City of Gothenburg's Department of Culture.

The museum primarily documents the stage work of the theatres of Gothenburg. The collection contains plays, posters, programmes, photographs, and items of scenography such as stage sets, costume sketches as well as stage models. The clippings archive contains reviews, biographies, and more, along with the Lorensberg Theatre's and the City of Gothenburg's Theatre's clippings archive. There are also archives of various theatre professionals.

Göteborgs universitetsbibliotek, Biblioteket för musik och dramatik

Gothenburg University Library, Music and Drama Library

POSTAL ADDRESS
Box 210
SE–405 30 Göteborg

CONTACT
+46 31 786 40 60
ubgumu@ub.gu.se
www.ub.gu.se/sv/bibliotek-och-oppettider/biblioteket-for-musik-och-dramatik

The library contains obligatory copies of works as well as archives and books of a number of theatre professionals connected with Gothenburg. Plays from Georg Wilhelm Berg's older theatres in Gothenburg, volumes 4–6 are available along with individual manuscripts by August Strindberg, plus Ebbe Linde's translations of foreign drama. Furthermore, Gustaf Bernström's collection of Ludvig Holberg's published writings, a collection of handwritten manuscripts with, among others, Arvid Englind's textbooks on Swedish and foreign plays of approximately 2400 volumes, and the archives of actors Maria Schildknecht and Helge Wahlgren, theatre directors Torsten Hammarén and Martin Sterner, plus Henrik Westin.

There are also audio and video recordings of theatre performances in Gothenburg as well as the Royal Dramatic Theatre in Stockholm. In addition, there are gramophone and tape recordings of both Swedish and foreign authors.

Gothenburg University is also involved in the research project EXPANSION OCH MÅNGFALD (Expansion and Diversity). A digital survey and analysis of the non-institutional performing arts in Gothenburg 1965–2000.

A more detailed description can be found on DIGIARVS homepage: www.digarv.se/deltagande-forskningsprojekt/expansion-och-mangfald.

Expansion's database can be found here: expansion.dh.gu.se.

Jussi Björlingmuseet

Jussi Björling Museum

POSTAL ADDRESS
Borganäsvägen 25
SE–784 33 Borlänge

CONTACT
+46 243 742 40
jussibjorlingmuseet@borlange.se
www.borlange.se/uppleva-och-gora/kultur/konst/jussi-bjorling

Konstakademien

The Royal Academy of the Arts

POSTAL ADDRESS
Box 163 17
SE–103 26 Stockholm

CONTACT
+46 8 23 29 45
biblioteket@konstakademien.se
www.konstakademien.se

The Royal Academy was founded by Gustav the 3rd during the second half of the 1700s. The Royal Academy of the Arts library is open to the public, while the archive can be visited by researchers by appointment. The collection contains books, paintings, and sculptures. Connections to the performing arts are in the form of set design sketches, architectural drawings, and engravings. Portraits and photographs from the 1870s and onward are also in the collection.

Kungliga biblioteket

The Royal Library of Sweden

POSTAL ADDRESS
Box 5039
SE–102 41 Stockholm

CONTACT
+46 10 709 30 00
info@kb.se
www.kb.se

The Royal Library is Sweden's national library. It has its origins in the royal Vasaäten family's book collection from the 1500 and 1600s. In 1877, the Royal Library became a public authority under the then Ecclesiastical Ministry, now, the Ministry of Education. The Library's mission is to promote Swedish research, science, and Swedish culture. The Library does this through collecting, describing, preserving, and providing anything that is printed and published in Sweden. Furthermore, its mission includes acquiring certain types of foreign literature, producing national bibliographic products, and supporting the Swedish library system in general through central initiatives.

Some of the collections concerning theatre historical material are: J. A. Hamilton's collection of English drama, the Huseby collection of English drama (1699 to the 1800s), Wilhelm Nylin's Strindberg collection, C. G. Tessin's and Oscar the 1st's collection of French drama, Vult von Steijern's Goethe and Wagner collection. There is also a collection of cuttings concerning theatres and theatre professionals.

Among the uncatalogued material are, among others, theatre posters, programmes, and various other pamphlets.

Books and printed material can be sought in Libris: libris.kb.se / Arkiv while personal archives can be sought in Arken: arken.kb.se.

Manuscripts, maps and pictures

The unit is responsible for collecting, acquiring, describing, preserving, and making available the Royal Library's collection of manuscripts, maps, and pictures, both published and non-published material.

The unit is also responsible for antiquarian acquisitions and for the publishing of music. Here, one can find, among other items, the Tessin collection with decorative engravings, as well as Arne Lindenbaum's and the Swedish Theatre Association's collection of portraits of actors.

In addition, some of the Royal Theatre's older documents can be found here along with the archives of Ludvig Josephson, F. A. Dahlgren, Nils Personne, Strindberg and Intima Theatre, as well as the Olof Molander and Molander family archives. Furthermore, duplicates of pamphlets from the Royal Dramatic Theatre and the Stockholm City Theatre are to be found here.

AUDIO-VISUAL COLLECTION

+46 10 709 30 20
forskarservice@kb.se

The Swedish media database SMDB, www.smdb.kb.se, is the search service fort he Royal Library's audio-visual collection. Here, one can find data about tv, radio, video, cinema films, records and computer games. This also includes tv and radio theaatre. SMDB covers most Swedish broadcasts and releases since 1979, but also includes even older material. Among others, one can find an almost complete register of Swedish gramaphone records from the end of the 1800s.

As opposed to the Royal Library's other collections, the audio-visual collection is only available for research purposes, and in order to use it, a user account is required.

Kungliga dramatiska teatern (Dramaten)

The Royal Dramatic Theatre

POSTAL ADDRESS
Nybroplan
SE–111 47 Stockholm

CONTACT
+46 8 667 06 80
kundservice@dramaten.se
www.dramaten.se

The Royal Dramatic Theatre, better known as Dramaten, is Sweden's national theatre and was founded in 1788 by Gustav the 3rd. Up until 1907, Dramaten was incorporated with the Royal Opera. Since 1908, Dramaten has been housed at Nybroplan (New Bridge Square) in Stockholm.

LIBRARY AND ARCHIVE
Box 5037
SE–102 41 Stockholm

CONTACT
+46 8 665 61 94
christine.sundberg@dramaten.se

The theatre's older documents can be found in the Royal Library's archives deposited at the Royal Opera at their premises in Gåddviken, Nacka. Documents concerning the theatre's activities after 1908 are kept, for the main part, at the theatre. Basically, there are two main parts: documents directly connected to the theatre's performances and documents connected to the theatre's administration. In the first part can be found, among others, a collection of plays, a photo archive, programme archive, press cuttings, and a collection of sheet music. In the second part can be found minutes of the theatre board's meetings, management correspondence, contracts of employment, documents concerning employee's salaries, and the theatre's accounts.

In the *Rollboken* www.dramaten.se/medverkande/rollboken it is possible to find production information about all of the theatre's productions since 1908.

Kungliga musikaliska akademien

The Royal Swedish Academy of Music

POSTAL ADDRESS
Blasieholmstorg 8
SE–111 48 Stockholm

CONTACT
+46 8 407 18 00
adm@musikaliskaakademien.se
www.musikaliskaakademien.se

The Academy was founded in 1771 by Gustav the 3rd and has as its mission the task of promoting and nurturing music as well as supporting education and research in the field of music. There is a close collaboration between the country's music and opera academies. The Academy's older archive (1771–1971) is deposited at the Music and Theatre Library at Statens Musikverk. It also includes the Academy of Music's archives until 1971. More recent archives are stored at the Academy.

The Academy runs the project Levende musikarv (The Living Music Legacy): levandemusikarv.se which aims to make available a large part of early Swedish music. The database contains information about music and musicians as well as sheet music which can be downloaded free of charge.

Kungliga operan

The Royal Swedish Opera

POSTAL ADDRESS
Jakobs torg 4
Box 16094
SE–103 22 Stockholm

CONTACT
+46 8 791 43 00
reception@operan.se
www.operan.se

The Royal Swedish Opera was founded in 1773 by Gustav the 3rd and was incorporated with the Royal Dramatic Theatre from its inception in 1788 until 1907.

THE OPERA'S COLLECTIONS AND ARCHIVE
+46 8 791 43 86
arkivet@operan.se

The archive contains administrative and artistic documents from recent years. In addition to the portrait collection, the art collection contains scenographic sketches and other pictorial material connected to the Royal Opera's history. The poster collection (1826–1942) is microfilmed and can also be found in paper copies.

There is also a costume collection and a collection of scenographic models by the scenographers Stellan Mörner, Kerstin Hedeby, Sven Erik Skawonius, Lars-Åke Thessman, and Lennart Mörk.

The repertoire database arkivet.operan.se/repertoar contains information about performances from 1773 up to today.

Kungliga Teatrarnas Arkiv (KTA)

The Royal Theatres' Archive

POSTAL ADDRESS
Kvarnholmsvägen 56
Gäddviken
SE–13131 Nacka

The Royal Theatres Archive contains documents appertaining to the Royal Opera (1773–1907) and the Royal Dramatic Theatre (1773–1907). The archive contains administrative and artistic material as well as printed items such as posters, business reports, and registers. The archive also contains a collection of approximately 2400 plays.

The theatre's older music collection is deposited with the The Royal Swedish Academy of Music at Statens Musikverk. More recent material is stored at the Royal Opera's Music Library.

Lunds universitetsbibliotek

Lund University Library

POSTAL ADDRESS
Helgonabacken 1
Box 3
SE–221 00 Lund

CONTACT
+46 46 222 91 90
info@ub.lu.se
www.ub.lu.se

The collection contains examples of Swedish printed works. The manuscript department houses the collection of scenographer Martin Ahlbom as well as the collection of August and Per Lindberg. There are also manuscripts and correspondence regarding Swedish authors.

Marionettmuseet

The Marionette Museum

Look for Statens musikverk, Musik- och teaterbiblioteket respektive Scenkonstmuseet.

Musik- och teaterbiblioteket

The Music and Theatre Library

Look for Statens musikverk.

Nationalmuseum

National Museum

POSTAL ADDRESS
Södra Blasieholmshamnen
Box 16176
SE–103 24 Stockholm

CONTACT
+46 8 519 543 00
info@nationalmuseum.se
www.nationalmuseum.se

The National Museum is Sweden's Art and Design Museum. The collections include paintings, sculptures, miniatures, handicrafts, designs, drawings, graphic sheets, and portrait photographs. In all, the collection consists of approximately 700,000 items from the 1500s up to today.

It also contains theatre related material in the form of, for example, the Tessin collection with French and Italian set decorations, and costume sketches, Swedish sketches from the1700s, architect drawings, along with Recueil Fossard (graphics with a Commedia dell'arte theme).

The National Museum also houses the Swedish portrait archive.

Nordiska museet

Nordic Museum

POSTAL ADDRESS
Djurgårdsvägen 6–16
Box 27820
SE–115 93 Stockholm

CONTACT
+46 8 519 546 00
info@nordiskamuseet.se
www.nordiskamuseet.se

The Nordic Museum is Sweden's largest cultural history museum. Other than documents concerning the museum's collection, the museum's archive also contains material related to the theatre and people connected with the theatre. For example, Strindbergiana in the form of letters, manuscripts, and photos, as well as documents regarding the Lövholm Theatre Company, and documents concerning Edvard Stjernström, Emil Roberg and Carl Grabow.

Regionarkivet, Västra Götalandsregionen och Göteborgs Stad

Regional Archives of Gothenburg

POSTAL ADDRESS
Box 2154
SE–403 13 Göteborg

CONTACT
+46 31 761 50 00
arkivnamnden@arkivnamnden.goteborg.se
www.goteborg.se/wps/portal?uri=gbglnk%3a201752131514651

Several archives of various theatres and theatre people in Gothenburg: Atelier Theatre, Gothenburg's Workers' Institute, The Central Box Office (Biljettcentralen) in Gothenburg AB, the Kortedala Model Theatre, theatre director August Lindberg, Gothenburgs Lyriska Theatre AB, the Lyriska Theatre's personnel assistance fund, The National Theatre, Nya Theatre, theatre director Albert Ranft, the City Commisioner's City Theatre Committee, the Gothenburg City Theatre, the Gothenburg City Theatre's Trust AB, the Restaurant (Restaurangen), the building committee for the refurbishment of the Stora Theatre, the Stora Theatre's pension and savings fund, Gothenburg Theatre AB, Gothenburg Theatre and Koncert Hall AB, the Theatre Historical Society in Gothenburg, Gothenburg's Theatre Museum (drawings).

Riksarkivet

The Swedish National Archives

POSTAL ADDRESS
Fyrverkarbacken 13–17
Box 125 41
SE–102 29 Stockholm

CONTACT
+46 10 476 70 00
riksarkivet@riksarkivet.se
www.riksarkivet.se

The National Archive is the highest governing authority within the public archive system. It is the archive governing authority, the archive depot, and the chief authority for the eight regional archives, and it superintends the national authorities' archive.

Archives with a connection to the theatre include, among others, the Dramatic Buildings Consortium's archive, Riksteatern's archive (from 1966), the Royal Swedish Academy of Music's archive (1771–1921). There are also diverse documents concerning the Royal Theatre. Furthermore, there are documents concerning the theatre in some of the archives belonging to individual members of the Swedish royal family.

The Swedish National Archive also administers the National Archive Database (NAD) sok.riksarkivet.se/nad in which it is possible to search archives from the whole of the country.

Scenkonstmuseet

Look for Statens musikverk.

Skissernas Museum

Museum of Artistic Process and Public Art

POSTAL ADDRESS
Finngatan 2
SE–223 62 Lund

CONTACT
+46 46 222 72 83
info@skissernasmuseum.lu.se
www.skissernasmuseum.se

The mission of the Museum of Artistic Process and Public Art is to collect sketches, models, and documentary material of art in a public environment. The collections include sketches and models for costumes and stage sets as well as of the permanent decor of theatre buildings. The documentary material also includes photos, slides, letters, and press clippings etc.

Statens musikverk

Swedish Performing Arts Agency

POSTAL ADDRESS
Box 16326
SE–103 26 Stockholm

CONTACT
+46 8 519 554 00
registrator@musikverket.se
www.musikverket.se

The Swedish Performing Arts Agency is an agency for the promotion and preservation of the cultural heritage of the performing arts and music. Its mission also includes giving economic support to various collaborative projects within the field of music. The Agency includes Caprice Records, the Electronic Musik Studio (EMS), the Music and Theatre Library of Sweden, the Music Platform (the handling of contributions), the Swedish Museum of Performing Arts as well as the Svenskt Visarkiv.

Musik- och teaterbiblioteket

The Music and Theatre Library of Sweden

POSTAL ADDRESS
Tegeluddsvägen 100
SE–115 28 Stockholm

CONTACT
+46 8 519 554 12
exp@musikverket.se
www.musikverket.se/musikochteaterbiblioteket

The library was founded in 2011 via the merger of the Music Library and the Swedish Theatre Museum. It is a specialist library for music, theatre, and dance. It includes sheet music and books regarding music and the performing arts in its broadest sense. In addition, there is a large collection of plays both published and via collected play manuscripts from Swedish theatres. The music section dates back to 1771, and the theatre section to 1922, which is reflected in the collections as they consist of both older and newer material.

The Marionette Museum's library is now a part of the Library's collection, and contains books on marionettes, shadow, and puppet theatre from all over the world.

The archive collections contain letters, published and administrative documents from various theatres and persons. In addition, there are photos and programmes. The Swedish Royal Theatre's music collection, which covers the period 1773 to the middle of the 1800s, is also deposited here.

The collection of press clippings mainly includes clippings from the Swedish press from 1860 to the year 2000.

There is also a register of performances in the form of an index card catalogue for Stockholm from 1863 and for Gothenburg from 1916, as well as for the whole of Sweden from about 1960 up to the beginning of the 2000s. Since 2007, theatre performances in Sweden have been registered in Scendatabasen www.scendatabasen.se which is run by the association Scensverige.

Some of the major theatre archives in the collection are the archives of Ludvig Josephson, Albert Ranft, Harald Molander, Gustaf Linden, Per Lindberg and Per Axel Branner.

Since 1966, the Library has published the journal *Dokumenterat* which, since 1995, has been available digitally: musikverket.se/musikochteaterbiblioteket/arkiv/dokumenterat. Every other issue contains an account of newly arrived dance, music, and theatre related material in Swedish archives and museums.

Scenkonstmuseet

The Swedish Museum of Performing Arts

POSTAL ADDRESS
Sibyllegatan 2
SE–103 26 Stockholm

CONTACT
+46 8 519 567 00
samling@scenkonstmuseet.se
www.scenkonstmuseet.se

The Swedish Museum of Performing Arts opened in 2017 and is a merger of the former Music Museum, Marionette Museum, and the Swedish Theatre Museum.

The museum's collections include approximately 6000 instruments. The music of the western world is well represented, especially the period 1600–1850. Here, one can also find a large collection of Swedish fold instruments, a large amount of instruments from the rest of Europe, and instruments from Asia and Africa.

The theatre collection includes stage sets, stage models, costumes and props, along with drawings and graphics in the form of décor and costume sketches, images of scenes and stage sets, and portraits from the 1500s and onward. Furthermore, there are costumes, diverse curiosities, and the remains of the Uppsala Old Theatre which comes from the Theatre Museum in Eskiltuna.

The photo archive mainly collects images of theatres, performances, and portraits. The Oreglia Collection is a collection of objects, masks, books, and paintings related to the Commedia dell'arte in various ways.

The puppet theatre collections consist of more than 4000 Swedish and foreign theatrical characters, sets, masks, animals, and props from the productions of the Marionette Theatre. There is also a large international collection, especially from Asia. A complete Wayang kulit theatre with 140 figures, bunraku puppets, and bunraku heads as well as unique Chinese hand puppets is also in the collection. Noticeable among the European collections are the Sicilian stick puppets, the Tunisian animal marionettes, and several works by well-known Swedish puppet makers.

Stiftelsen Ingmar Bergman

The Ingmar Bergman Foundation

POSTAL ADDRESS
Borgvägen 1–5
Box 27178
SE–102 52 Stockholm

CONTACT
+46 8 665 11 00
info@ingmarbergman.se
www.ingmarbergman.se

The foundation's purpose is to manage the archive of Ingmar Bergman as well as to promote an understanding of Bergman and his art. The archive is not open to the general public, but can be made available to researchers for research purposes.

Stiftelsen Musikkulturens Främjande

The Nydahl Collection

POSTAL ADDRESS
Riddargatan 35–37
SE–114 57 Stockholm

CONTACT
+46 8 661 71 71
smf@nydahlcoll.se
www.nydahlcoll.se

The foundation has a collection of about 600 instruments which are on permanent display. The collections include musical autographs, letters and other documents, and a collection of books on various music and musicians. In addition, there are theatre almanacs, pictures and posters, as well as most of Ingmar Bengtsson's library and manuscripts.

Stockholms stadsarkiv

Stockholm City Archive

POSTAL ADDRESS
Kungsklippan 6
Box 22063
SE–104 22 Stockholm

CONTACT
+46 8 508 283 00
stadsarkivet@stockholm.se
www.stadsarkivet.stockholm.se

Here, one can find archive material on, among others, Humlegårds Theatre, Ladugård's Regional Theatre (Folkteatern), Mindre Theatre (Hammerska Barn), Nya Theatre, Olympia Theatre (Östermalm's Theatre), and Södra Theatre. There are also the personal archives of Erik af Edholm, Johan Flodmark, Anders Lindeberg and A. F. Ristell.

Stockholms stadsmuseum

Stockholm City Museum

POSTAL ADDRESS
Box 15025
SE–104 65 Stockholm

CONTACT
+46 8 508 316 20
stadsmuseet@stockholm.se
www.stadsmuseet.stockholm.se

The museum's purpose is to illustrate the municipality's origin and development. This also includes the city's cultural heritage.

The archives include, among others, Atelier Jaeger (Herman Sylvander's collection) as well as Almberg and Preinitz' collection of theatre negatives. There are also theatre posters and drawings. Malmsten's circus, variety, and theatre collection is also stored here with portraits of actors and posters from Stockholm theatres 1830–1930.

Strindbergsmuseet

The Strindberg Museum

POSTAL ADDRESS
Drottninggatan 85
SE–111 60 Stockholm

CONTACT
+46 8 411 53 54
info@strindbergsmuseet.se
www.strindbergsmuseet.se

The Strindberg Museum's collections contain items that have a direct connection to August Strindberg and his immediate family, along with how producers and reproducers of Strindberg have interpreted his works in various ways.

The collections contain books, programmes, posters, photographs, and various other objects. There is also an extensive press cuttings archive which, among other things, includes a complete collection of reviews of Swedish productions of Strindberg's plays.

Svenska filminstitutet

Swedish Film Institute

POSTAL ADDRESS
Filmhuset
Borgvägen 1–5
Box 27 126
SE–102 52 Stockholm

CONTACT
+46 8 665 11 00
registrator@filminstitutet.se
www.filminstitutet.se

The Swedish Film Institute's purpose is to support the production of new films as well as to distribute and show films of worth, and to preserve and make available the heritage of Swedish films. In the library and archive, there are films, film manuscripts, programmes, posters, and both film company and personal archives.

Teaterförbundet för scen och film

The Swedish Union for Performing Arts and Film

POSTAL ADDRESS
Kaplansbacken 2 A
Box 12710
SE–112 94 Stockholm

CONTACT
+46 8 441 13 00
info@teaterforbundet.se
www.teaterforbundet.se

Teatermuseet, scen- och manegekonst

The Theatre Museum

POSTAL ADDRESS
Kalendergatan 5C
SE–211 35 Malmö

CONTACT
+46 40 12 48 83
www.teatermuseet.com

The museum's goal is to preserve and document the history and traditions of the theatre and performing arts. The collections focus are on the south of Sweden, and include, among other things, photographs and archive material from the majority of Scanian theatres from the 1800s and on. There is a large amount of material on Edvard Persson, and the museum has a permanent exhibition on Nils Poppe.

Uppsala universitetsbibliotek, Carolina Rediviva

Uppsala University Library

POSTAL ADDRESS
Dag Hammarskjölds väg 1
Box 510
SE–751 20 Uppsala

CONTACT
+46 18 471 39 00
fraga.biblioteket@ub.uu.se
www.ub.uu.se

The library has collections of letters and documents concerning several Swedish authors and playwrights. In addition, there is the personal archive of Gustav the 3rd and the so called Düben collection with music and opera notes from the 1600 and 1700s.

The search page for the reservation of items can be found here: uppsala.libsurveys.com/loader.php?id=30735d1cbb0c0c733e1cd856406f7c30.

There are also portraits, drawings, and topographical pictures appertaining to various theatres, along with photographer, Nils Gunnar Sundgrens documentation of Uppsala's old theatre.

Universities of the performing arts' and the Theatre Academy's educational and masters' courses

Göteborgs universitet

University of Gothenburg

POSTAL ADDRESS
Box 100
SE–405 30 Göteborg

VISITOR ADDRESS
Universitetsplatsen 1
SE–411 24 Göteborg

CONTACT
031–786 00 00
registrator@gu.se
www.gu.se

Högskolan för scen och musik

Academy of Music and Drama

POSTAL ADDRESS
Box 210
SE–405 30 Göteborg

VISITOR ADDRESS
Fågelsången 1
SE–412 56 Göteborg

CONTACT
serviceexpedition@hsm.gu.se
www.hsm.gu.se

Institutionen för litteratur, idéhistoria & religion, Teaterstudier

Department of Literature, History of Ideas, and Religion, Theatre Studies

POSTAL ADDRESS
Box 200
SE–405 30 Göteborg

VISITOR ADDRESS
Lundgrensgatan 1B
SE–412 56 Göteborg

CONTACT
+46 31 78 61 115
lir@lir.gu.se
www.lir.gu.se

Luleå tekniska universitet

Luleå University of Technology

POSTAL ADDRESS
SE–971 87 Luleå

CONTACT
+46 92 04 91 000
registrator@ltu.se
www.ltu.se

Teaterhögskolan i Luleå

Theatre Academy

VISITOR ADDRESS
Universitetsområdet
SE–972 39 Luleå

CONTACT
+46 92 04 92 846
teaterhogskolan@ltu.se
www.ltu.se/ltu/Kontakta-oss/Lulea/Teaterhogskolan

Lunds universitet

Lund University

POSTAL ADDRESS
Box 117
SE–221 00 Lund

CONTACT
+46 222 00 00
lu@lu.se
www.lu.se

Språk- och litteraturcentrum

Centre for Languages and Literature

POSTAL ADDRESS
Box 201
SE–221 00 Lund

CONTACT
+46 222 32 10
reception@sol.lu.se
www.sol.lu.se/teater

Teaterhögskolan i Malmö

Malmö Theatre Academy

POSTAL ADDRESS
Box 8100
SE–200 41 Malmö

VISITOR ADDRESS
Bergsgatan 31
SE–21422 Malmö

CONTACT
+46 40 32 55 65
thm@thm.lu.se
www.thm.lu.se

Stockholms konstnärliga högskola (SKH)

Stockholm University of the Arts

POSTAL ADDRESS
Box 24045
SE–104 50 Stockholm

VISITOR ADDRESS
Linnégatan 87
SE–115 23 Stockholm

CONTACT
+46 8 49 400 000
registrator@uniarts.se
www.uniarts.se

Stockholm University of the Arts includes a circus, dance, opera and theatre academy.

DOCH, Dans- och cirkushögskolan

VISITOR ADDRESS
Brinellvägen 58
SE–114 28 Stockholm

CONTACT
www.uniarts.se/om-skh/
doch-dans-och-cirkushogskolan

Operahögskolan

VISITOR ADDRESS
Teknikringen 35
SE–114 28 Stockholm

CONTACT
www.uniarts.se/om-skh/operahogskolan

Stockholms dramatiska högskola

VISITOR ADDRESS
Valhallavägen 189
SE–115 53 Stockholm

CONTACT
www.uniarts.se/om-skh/
stockholms-dramatiska-hogskola

Stockholms universitet

Stockholm University

POSTAL ADDRESS
Universitetsvägen 10 A
SE–106 91 Stockholm

CONTACT
+46 8 16 20 00
registrator@su.se
www.su.se

Institutionen för kultur och estetik, Teatervetenskap

Department for Culture and Aesthetics

POSTAL ADDRESS
Frescativägen 22B–26
SE–106 91 Stockholm

CONTACT
registrator.ike@su.se
www.su.se/ike/teatervetenskap

Örebro universitet

Örebro University

POSTAL ADDRESS
Fakultetsgatan 1
SE–702 81 Örebro

CONTACT
+46 19 30 30 00
registrator@oru.se
www.oru.se

Musikhögskolan, Teaterpedagogik

School of Music, Theatre and Art

POSTAL ADDRESS
Gymnastikgatan 1
SE–701 82 Örebro

CONTACT
+46 19 30 30 00
mh@oru.se
www.oru.se/institutioner/musikhogskolan

Index

Index

Index